CHECKING

INTO

FAITH

Personal and Group

Study Guide Included

By Ian Green

Study Guide by Nicki Straza

Brilliant! In "Checking into Faith" Ian Green has combined inspiring faith building stories with possibly the best explanation of faith I have ever read. As you read, you will discover the vision God has for your life and understand how to lay hold of God's provision. These principles of faith and how they operate in relationship to one another will equip people in practical ways to live and walk an adventurous life of faith.

Bruce Friesen
Founder of Lifetree Church & Ministries, of Transform Your World and of Children Arise

We have had the privilege of knowing Ian and Judith for almost three decades. This script is filled with true life encounters of a modern day ambassador of new testament faith. His passion to see faith increased in believers is highly contagious. Ian has modelled the message that he writes. This subject, faith, sets him apart to be one of today's signature influencers in Christ's body. We highly value Ian's legacy of a faith-filled life through his writings. Enjoy the read, but be careful, its contents when fully imbibed could cause permanent life change.

Kenn & Cheryl
Ripple Effect Ministries and Network - Focused on participating in the full restoration of an apostolic Christianity in the earth.

Ian Green has always been a man who practices what he preaches and who puts action into his faith. In this inspiring book, Ian stirs us to step out of our comfort zones and into the amazing adventure God has for each one of us. Highly recommended!

Mark Conner
Senior Minister of City Life Church in Melbourne, Australia

Ian Green is a life time friend and encourager. Wherever Ian goes he is a catalyst for change and for an increase in faith. I know this book will bless and encourage your faith and be a catalyst for forward momentum in your journey with God.

Brent Cantelon
Evangelist/Missionary Pentecostal Assemblies of Canada

Having known Ian for many years now, "Checking into Faith" is born out of both his experience, passion and love for the Church. I would thoroughly recommend this book as an excellent read for all.

John Partington
Former National Leader of Assemblies of God Great Britain

Ian Green is man who just doesn't speak about faith, he lives it. Over the years, Ian's radical obedience to God has seen the transformational power of God released on the earth. This book will inspire and empower you to start to live your own journey of faith. I thoroughly recommend you read this book.

Russell Evans
Founder and Senior Pastor of Planetshakers Ministries and Churches

This is a book about faith written by a man who lives by faith. Its aim is not to do with more 'information' about the subject but it is to do with 'formation' of a person's life. Readers can expect an impartation of the Holy Spirit. Ian's faith is actually contagious.

Stuart Bell
Senior Pastor of Alive Church and leader of the Ground Level network.

The book you are holding in your hands talks about the author exactly in the way I know him. You will read about faith and miracles with a humour only Ian can come up with. In case you do not know Ian - he is the person who visited me in 1997 in my newly launched church with only 30 people in the service. And right there he asked me a question that changed my life forever: "Stanislav, what if next year you would plant another 15 churches in around cities with these 30 people you have here?" It did not happen that year but it did happen eventually. Thanks to the courage and faith of this godly man I am leading a movement of 30 churches in the Czech Republic nowadays, and all together we have 1000 people each and every week in our Sunday services. This book is as dangerous as its author. Be careful with reading - it may happen that your life will not be the same after finishing this book!

Stanislav Bubik
Apostolic Founder and Leader of No Boundaries Churches

Passion with strategic purpose. Inspiration with Kingdom insight. These phrases summarise my experience with Ian Green. Around the globe there are thousands of people like me who have had the course of the lives inexorably changed through relationship with Ian. His hunger for the Lord combines with a limitless desire to see people discover their place in God's transformational work. His life's journey continues to challenge me, his friendship continues to strengthen me, and his faith continues to call me to new places in God.

Bill Howell
Director at Roma Learning to Fly

If you have ever wondered how to move your faith from wishful thinking to reality, this book is for you. *In-your-face* and *give-it-a-go* style of ministry and leadership is status quo with Ian Green. Ian's influence in my life and countless others was ground-breaking, and captured the imagination of a generation of young Christians. Ian Green has something to say, and it is worth our while to listen!

Jamie Stewart
Lead Pastor – Life Church, Kissimmee, FL

Focused on leadership dynamics and community practices in multicultural churches that promote spiritual formation and global influence. It has been my privilege to know Ian and Judith Green for nearly 15 years. Every time we are together, without exception, I leave encouraged and inspired to seek the kingdom of God first and give my life fully to His mission. Ian has the gift of encouragement calling out faith and courage in all followers of Jesus. He has inspired thousands of Canadian leaders to ignore the lies of negativity and dream about what is possible for those who live by faith. He has led by example and has modelled the biblical principles of faith, obedience and courage. I am glad he has taken the time to put pen to paper to share his journey and thoughts in this inspired book. Bringing the good news to the unreached world is not for the faint of heart. It is for the courageous and obedient and Ian's faith experiences will help encourage many in the journey.

Murray Cornelius
Executive Director, International Missions, The Pentecostal Assemblies of Canada - Mobilising the church to fulfil the Mission of God.

Ian Green is a man of deep conviction and untamed dreams. As you read this book, you will discover faith boosting testimonies that can release God's potential in your own life and ministry. Get ready to be inspired to live fully alive in God's world and for God's glory.

Andy Moore
Lead Pastor, GT Church

As a writer, justice fighter and pastor, this is a must read. "Checking into Faith" will be a go-to-guide for many years to come. I have been constantly challenged in the last few days by Ian's words in the opening salvo of his book, "When the wall came down in east Berlin in 1989, I kept saying "someone has to go into Eastern Europe and DO SOMETHING." Faith is once again rising in my heart and it's time to act. Better days ahead.

Anthony Liebenberg
Founder of Life Child and Senior Pastor of Life Church
Author of 'Facing Forward', 'Big God Big Life' & 'Winning
Life'.www.lifechild.org.za and www.life-church.co.za

Ian Green, and his wife Judith, have lived a life of uncomplicated faith. In a world where academics can give us their theories, Ian shares his life with us; it has been one of truth and experience that has not only empowered him to do the impossible, but has impassioned hundreds of leaders to do likewise. His stories are those of an authentic disciple who has known tragedies and triumphs, mountaintops and deep valleys, but whose faith has become stronger through them all. Because of the generosity of Ian's heart, and the message he carries, churches have been planted, communities transformed, and nations impacted. He is a man of integrity and strong convictions and one that I have grown to love and value as a true friend. I highly recommend his book and believe that it has enormous value to a generation that desperately needs to rediscover true biblical faith.

David McCracken
David McCracken Ministries
www.davidmccracken.org

We all have chances to check out faith. George Mueller of Bristol with only two shillings (50 cents) in his pocket started a work to support Christian schools, assist missionaries and give away Bibles. Without asking anyone, committees, subscribers or memberships *through faith in the Lord alone* for help he got and gave more than one and a half million pounds (then $7,500,000). His schools trained 122,000 kids; he sent out some 282,000 Bibles and 1,500,000 New Testaments, produced 112 million books tracts and materials for missionaries all over the world. He also kept some ten thousand children clothed and fed who had no parents or homes and for sixty-four years saw the power and grace of God at work to bless, provide for and keep them. *They never missed a meal.* What would you think of a faith that at the age of 70 sent him in 17 years of evangelism 200,000 miles around the world, preaching often to as many as 4,500-5,000 people in many lands in several different languages until he was ninety to some three million people? How? By faith. My friend Ian has had his times to test it out himself and tell us what he found. Now it's our turn.

Winkie Pratney
Author, speaker, evangelist and Christian apologist
www.winkiepratney.net/
Auckland, New Zealand

I have known Ian Green for longer than most. We met as young, naïve College students, shared a room for a year and shared some of the earliest faith journeys together. We laughed much, prayed together and then would speak for hours about our shared passion to make Jesus known around the earth. Over forty years later some of these things have not changed – we still laugh much, talk often and, most important of all, have a passion to bring the good news of Jesus to all. So, I heartily endorse this book. It was Ian who first inspired me into generous living and giving and it will be his stories in this book that will do the same. Get it, read it, and let the narratives of faith deeply impact your life.

Paul R Alexander, PhD
Global pilgrim, passionate missionary and President, Trinity Bible College and Graduate School, Ellendale, ND

If ever someone has put their life message into book form my friend and ministry colleague, Ian Green has done this in "Checking into Faith". Ian has always inspired me to be a leader who sees with God-sized vision and then to pursue that with passionate abandonment and obedience. It is a gift to have him put the biblical principles that he and Judith have lived by into words illustrated with numerous examples from their own faith-filled, generous lives. This book served as a mirror for my own life as I evaluated my current walk of faith and was challenged to trust God for all that He has in mind for me and those I serve in the days ahead.

Rev. Dr. David Wells
General Superintendent of The Pentecostal Assemblies of Canada

The journey of faith is one of stretching, growth and exciting adventures. Over the past 30 years that I have known Ian Green, I have watched him walk this journey. He is a man of faith. "Checking into Faith" is a book that outlines principles of faith which are backed up with authentic life experiences. As you read of another man's experiences, you will be challenged and inspired to carve out your own walk of faith – to leave a legacy that others can follow.

Wayne Alcorn
National President of Australian Christian Churches

Ian Green is larger than life. He actually believes in changing the world. His faith will shake you to the core. His enthusiasm will affect you for the long haul. His heart will provoke you to become a better person. His sound teaching will force you to surrender. I was brought to tears reading some of the stories he encountered amongst the poorest in Eastern Europe. When it comes to faith, Ian is no superficial and easy blabber – he will take you to the deep places of the journey to God's heart.

Alain Caron
Leader of the Hodos Network
Author of Apostolic Centers

Table of Contents

Acknowledgements

We all have a story to tell. Some of our experiences need other people to help us articulate what has happened in our lives. This book has been greatly helped by the four editors that have freely given their time and literary expertise. Many thanks to Greg Foley, Karma Pratt, Judith Green and master editor Mark Griffin.

This second edition includes a personal and group study guide. Many thanks to Nicki Straza for her work on this.

This is a book of many stories. All the stories have connected parts and include many different characters. My journey of faith has involved many who have contributed to it.

The list is long and I am not attempting to list them all, but I am eternally grateful for the richness of faith that they deposited into my life.

The person who pointed the way and led me to Jesus – Andy Watkins.

My first pastor, who taught me the basics of the Christian walk and laid a foundation that was solid in both the Spirit and the Word – Paul Mercy.

My first Mentor and Discipler who taught me how to read the Bible and pray – Hayden Howells.

I am deeply grateful for the numerous friends and colleagues around me that modelled faith at an extraordinary level. Books and authors that have inspired me for four decades and the communities of faith that have assisted me in my spiritual formation. There is not enough space to write all of these names down.

I am thankful for the incredibly dark moments, when it seemed all was lost and the light of hope appeared as faith rose in my heart.

My wife, Judith, through the most challenging moments of my life, encouraged me to press on to what God had in store for us. This is a walk I never could have done on my own.

My children Sophie and Morgan have seen me in my brightest days as well as in moments of seeming defeat. Their encouragement, prayer and the releasing of their outrageous father has been both remarkable and gracious.

Finally, all thanks must go to the Author and Finisher of our faith Jesus Christ who has been faithful, trustworthy and consistent. Truly, I am one grateful man.

Preface

There seems to be a recurring theme in the things that God has placed in my heart. The repetitive refrains of faith will grow like Topsy over the course of weeks or months; inescapable, unavoidable ideas, even if they seem impossible. Standing strong behind these incredible notions are the supporting girders of faith – the redundant motivator that is continually popping up everywhere I turn. It has become, over the last four decades, a core calling in almost everything that I do in my life.

When the wall came down in east Berlin in 1989, I kept saying "someone has to go into Eastern Europe and DO SOMETHING." No one seemed to be doing much for the gospel, yet hundreds of other companies were setting up shop on the other side of the crumbled wall, especially the dodgiest of businesses pedalling their wares, and some of them had their business plans being implemented within 48 hours. At that point, this thing started to grow in my heart that maybe I needed to do something. Should I be the one to walk away from my secure job, a steady income, a stable life? That wouldn't make sense would it? How could I do something? What could I do to make a difference? How could that possibly help? But, along came faith. Unfortunately!

Faith changes everything. Faith won't let me sit in my recliner every evening and watch television. Faith keeps stirring me to believe and do things that are utterly impossible.

Some friends have said, many actually, that they suspect I have a "gift" of faith. I don't go around telling others that, but apparently, they keep hearing it come out of my mouth and then seeing it in action all over my life. My poor wife has been dragged along in this wild ride that God and faith have taken us on, but she has been more than a good sport – I think she might actually enjoy this wild ride of faith! She has seen the benefits, the payoff for the seemingly senseless risks we have taken. I see in her and many others that faith is radically contagious.

I believe that God has used my outlandish faith to inspire an ability to believe in others, to believe for fundamentally crazy things that they have never before thought possible.

Friends and colleagues have been after me for years saying "you need to write down some of those stories and thoughts about faith". I suppose that through these friends I also have that nagging sense that God might just being suggesting the same thing. Over the course of the last few decades, we've stumbled forward into some things that might be of help to others. Many of these concepts have found their way into messages, not just more sermons, but a huge part of my life story that I am passionate about.

These messages have been transcribed, adapted and retooled into book form.

In this edition, I have invited Nicki Straza to develop a personal and group study guide that can help you take these messages from information to transformation in your journey of faith.

I certainly don't have the faith journey entirely figured out, but I pray that these stories and thoughts would profoundly encourage and be catalytic in provoking the next levels of faith in every reader.

I believe they will.

Using the Study Guide

For Groups

Each chapter includes a review and highlight from the book chapter to open your weekly group session followed by group discussion questions. Take time to allow each person to share as they feel comfortable and use the journal prompts and call to action as ways for your group to remain engaged throughout the week. Following up the next week on what the members learned and followed through with during the week encourages both accountability and vulnerability, two keys to growing our faith. As a leader, be sure to do the work yourself so you can share in the journey with those in your group. God will highlight something new every time.

For Individuals

Each chapter includes a personal reflection section that also has journal prompts that you can use throughout the week to explore and discover more richly what God is wanting to say to you through this book.

Keeping a notebook handy is a great way to keep track and review what God lays on your heart.

This is Ground Control

Throughout this study guide you will be challenged to press in and be still to listen for the still small voice of the Holy Spirit as He speaks to you. Take time to pray and invite the Lord to speak to you as you read the book chapters and challenge yourself with the questions. Trust that He will lead you and record the thoughts and ideas that bubble up. In the flight of faith, the voice of God is our ground control, our anchor, and our guide.

Pre-Flight Checklist

Before you jump into this study guide lets consider what elements will make your experience most effective.

Accountability: It will be tempting to go through this alone, but having a partner or a small group to do this with adds a depth and richness that you will value for years to come. Be encouraged to invite someone to hold you accountable to the things you are learning so that this journey becomes transformation not just information in your life.

Journaling: Whether as an individual or in groups, taking notes of insights, ideas, and revelations will give you something to refer back to. Journal your prayers to God and then keep writing as Holy Spirit speaks back to you.

Experimenting: Unless you begin to test the ideas shared in this book, the words will settle down as information and your life will remain the same. Experiment, be curious, dare to believe God at His word. Your faith muscles will begin to stretch and grow strong and you will find yourself being transformed!

Choosing: The incredible thing about faith is you only need a mustard seed and a choice. Your faith will grow as you align your choices with God's word. Will you to take flight?

Flight Instructions

Flight Plan: A quick review of the main themes of the chapter.

Take-Off: A closer look at a significant story or analogy from the chapter.

Flight Crew: Group discussion questions.

Captain's Log: Personal reflection questions and journal prompts.

In-Flight Training: Take action by defining and practicing a step of obedience and walking it out in faith.

Checking IN or Checking OUT?: Evaluate honestly where you are. Anticipate the tactics of the enemy. Recalibrate where necessary.

Ground Control: Jesus is the ultimate navigator, seeking to know, hear, and respond to His voice and be quick to obey is key to checking into faith. Be intentional to set aside time for prayer and listening.

Soaring Higher: Want to investigate more? You will find resources and challenges to take your faith to new heights with God!

What is Faith?

People have all kinds of strange ideas about faith. Some people think that faith is on the same plateau as the Tooth Fairy, the Easter Bunny, and Santa Claus. Some people believe that faith is a fantasy, on the level of non-rational thinking. I do not believe that. I believe that faith is rational, it is substantial, and it is concrete.

Hebrews 11:1 gives us the Bible's definition of faith. "Faith is the confidence that what we hope for will actually happen; it gives us assurance about things we cannot see."[1] Do you have that? Hebrews 11:6 tells us "...it is impossible to please God without faith." To bring pleasure to God is the exact opposite of the enemy's intention for our lives.

Consequently, faith – the five letter F-word – is the vilest of language in Satan's vocabulary.

Hebrews 4:2 says, "For we also had the gospel preached to

us just as they did, but the message they heard was of no value to them because those who heard it did not combine *it with faith."* If we take the gospel message, mix it with faith, and apply it to our lives, we experience the explosion of substance to move forward in the kingdom of God. Faith is an attitude. It is absolutely impossible to have negative attitudes and positive faith.

Faith is an Attitude

Faith is the attitude by which we receive the Word of God into our hearts. Faith responds readily by acting in keeping with what God has already said. The Bible talks about the word of faith that came to Israel, and how the negative attitude of the Israelites caused them to refuse to enter into the Promised Land.

Hebrews 4 says, *"It remains that some will enter the rest. Those formerly had the gospel preached to them and did not go in because of their disobedience."* You may ask, "What does disobedience have to do with faithlessness?" Two Greek words in the Bible are translated *unbelief.* The first word is *apistia,* which means "faithless, unfaithfulness, or weakness of faith." The second word is *apeitheia,* which means "obstinacy, obstinate opposition to the divine will, or a stubborn refusal to believe or to act."

The people of God had an opportunity to move into the Promised Land. It was there waiting for them, their name was on the deed, but the Bible says they obstinately refused to agree with God and stubbornly disobeyed the command of God. It is possible to refuse faith. Even as you read, faith is percolating in your heart, and you have an opportunity to either refuse faith or receive faith.

The Bible says Christians have received a *measure of faith.*[2] It is already deposited inside of us.

What we should do is work with that faith, and walk forward to whatever God is telling us to do. Some years ago, I was traveling from Gdansk in Northern Poland toward Wroclaw in Southern Poland. I had to change trains mid-journey and got off the train to grab a Polish cup of coffee—the type guaranteed to keep you awake for the next three weeks! Pure Undiluted Caffeine. I got back on the train carrying my suitcase and briefcase. As I was walking down the corridor toward my seat, these big brutes, smelling drunk as skunks, started hassling and pushing me. I got to my seat and discovered that my wallet was gone. I had been pickpocketed. I started shouting, "I've been robbed. I've been robbed!" But no one was taking a blind bit of notice.

Eventually the ticket lady appeared, so I told her what had happened. She asked me how long ago it had been, and I told her it had happened only about two minutes ago. She replied, "Oh, if it is that long ago, those boys are long gone." She told me to report the robbery at the police station in Wroclaw.

I stood in the corridor and was definitely not full of the joy of the Lord. I was thinking about the hassle ahead: getting my birth certificate faxed through, getting my tickets reissued, and cancelling my credit cards. And then there was the $300 U.S. I thought I would never see again. As I was standing in the corridor thinking these happy thoughts, a word came into my heart: "You have been blessed." Like good Polish sausage, the word kept repeating. I started to agree with the word—my name has been written in heaven and my future is good. I was not enjoying what had just happened, but I WAS blessed. I began to confess the word in my heart and get it out of my mouth. Suddenly an infusion of faith came inside of me. I said, "God, You know where that wallet is. You can send Your angel Gabriel down from heaven, jump on those boys, beat them up, and get my wallet!"

As I was praying this outrageous prayer, a man came walking down the corridor toward me carrying something that looked a lot like my wallet. "That's my wallet!" I said. He replied,

"Are you sure?" He pulled out my picture and said, "Yeah, it looks like it is. The bad news is there is no money in it so you can't even buy me a beer!" For me, that was an opportunity to receive faith or to reject faith. Opportunities like this come to each of us. We have the vote. We decide how to respond to situations and circumstances. Faith is an attitude.

Faith is an Action

Faith is also an action; it is never passive. James 2:17- 18 says, "In the same way, faith by itself, if not accompanied by actions, is dead. And some will say, 'You have faith, I have deeds.' Show me your faith without your deeds and I will show you my faith by what I do." Faith is active. Some people ask about that passage in the Old Testament where Israel is trapped against the Red Sea and Moses declares, "Stand still and see the salvation of the Lord." They were not standing still because they did not know what to do. They were standing still, believing that deliverance would come.

They were activating their faith—they were looking for the LORD to bring deliverance. They had an active faith. Faith in action provokes God to action.

Hebrews 11 is not just a bunch of interesting stories; it is about a gang of people who show us how to activate faith. There are three definitive conditions for faith to be activated. First, we must know what God has said. Second, we have to be radically obedient to what God has said. Third, we must continue in what God has said.

For the most part, God speaks to me through the Bible, probably 95 per cent of the times that I hear His voice. Occasionally, I get a prophetic word, or an impulse, or a gut feeling, but largely I get direction through the Bible. When you understand that God has spoken, it is presumption to go *beyond* what God has said. It is unbelief not to *go as far* as God has said. It is an expression of disobedience if we *go against* what God has said.

Faith is an agreement with what God is saying, causing us to act in line with what God has said. God's Word is God's Word; we can be confident in that.

Faith is Obedience

It is imperative that we obey the Word of God that we have received. You can receive information, but you still have to be obedient. We have been planting churches down in Serbia and it is challenging terrain. We have planted six or seven churches, and many of the people we have been working with are from a gypsy movement. One church has grown from 40 to 1,000 people over a seven-year period. We encouraged that church to plant more churches. They identified and equipped four or five church planters and sent them out.

One of the new leaders, Miro, had a simple faith and was passionate about Jesus. He went down to a city and began to look for a "man of peace."[3]

He hunted around the city and found a man by the name of Vladimir, who had been unemployed and was in a poor state. He visited this man on and off for six or seven days and eventually, the man came to Jesus. Miro was thrilled and excited and told him that Jesus had forgiven him. He also said, "Jesus can heal your emphysema. I'm going to pray for you."

After three days, all the pain across Vladimir's chest had lifted. He was so excited that he went outside and began to run up and down the street showing sufficient evidence that Jesus had healed him. Miro did not stop there. He said to Vladimir, "We need to pray that you get your job back." Vladimir replied, "I'll never get my job back. There is 92 per cent unemployment, I am a gypsy, and there is a fair amount of racial tension." They prayed for 10 days and then came a knock on the door from the manager of the factory. The manager had heard that Vladimir was feeling much better; he wanted to know if he wanted his job back. Hallelujah! It took radical obedience combined with simple faith to advance the kingdom of God.

That is all God will demand of us.

Having received the word, and having been obedient, we may think it is all over; our job is finished. However, we may then discover what the Apostle Peter learned that dark night on the Sea of Galilee. He heard the word, he was obedient to the word, and he got out of the boat only to find that things got worse. When we step out of the boat of our security and begin to exercise faith, we should continue in faith and hold firmly to what God has said.

There may be delays, there may be contradictions, discouragements or adverse circumstances, but none of those should override what God has said. You have to keep moving forward.

Daniel is a church planter in Poland. He lived in northern Poland but felt moved to participate in a project that was in southern Poland. He told me that God wanted him to be a part of the project, but he had one difficulty—he could not sell his apartment and needed to do so before he could rent one down south.

The challenge was that his apartment had been up for sale for seven years and it had not sold. Daniel said, "I'm going to fast and pray until God sells my apartment." On the 32nd day of his fast, God broke into his life. He sold his apartment for a load of cash—so much so that when he moved down south he did not buy an apartment, he bought a primary school.

Daniel began to renovate a part of the school for his family to live in. But there were also many homeless people in the city and he started to reach out to them. The mayor of the city was so impressed by what Daniel was doing that he offered him financial support. This was not normal—a Polish government official helping a Protestant church. Later, the mayor went to a mayor's convention and he began to brag about Daniel and the work that he was doing. Other mayors started contacting Daniel and he subsequently started 20 more centres across Poland paid for by government funds.

The Swedish government heard about what Daniel was doing in Poland and they began flying him up to Stockholm to confer with the Interior Minster regarding how to best deal with homeless people.

When you get the word of the Lord, when you understand the word of the Lord, you have to be obedient to the word of the Lord. However, you must continue in faith until you get to the end of the road and the goodness and the glory of God are manifested.

Faith is Agreement

Jesus made an astonishing statement when He said, "Again, I tell you that if two of you agree on earth about anything you ask, it will be done by My Father in heaven."[4] Paul said, "No matter how many promises God has made, they are yes in Jesus Christ."[5] Faith is an agreement. Agreement can work both negatively and positively. If you believe you can, you can and if you believe you can't, you can't. Faith will always reach its objective.

The twelve spies went into the Promised Land, checked things out and came back. Ten of them said, "We can't do it." They had faith to believe they couldn't do it, and they didn't. Two of them said, and this is a loose translation, "Put a sock in it, guys! We can go in and wallop those giants and we can take the land."

Caleb and Joshua said, "We can do it", and they did it.[6]

If you believe you can, you can; if you believe you can't, you can't. You decide what you want. Faith is a powerful agreement. When we agree with God, or sometimes with another brother, we can go in and take the land.

Faith is Assurance

Faith is an assurance: "Let us go near to God with a sincere heart in full assurance of faith, having our hearts sprinkled to cleanse us from a guilty conscience, having our bodies washed with pure water." Faith is an assurance. True faith does not allow doubt to achieve its objective. It does not waver. It does not divide confidence. Faith is an agreement with what God has spoken; therefore, have faith means being able to act with assurance.

Some years ago, I had a car and it died. I laid hands on it, anointed it with oil, cursed it, blessed it, took authority over it, and pushed it to the garage. I was working for Youth Alive UK driving 60-70,000 kilometres per year and I needed a vehicle. One of my co-workers told me I could import a car from Belgium and with a 25 per cent discount, it would only cost £4,000. That sounded challenging then because that was two years' salary. It was not that the car was expensive, but I was on a very low salary. I do not mind fasting, but two years without food seemed a little extreme.

I asked Jesus what I should do and I felt He was saying, "I want you to go for it."

Many times, when we have the challenge of faith, we ask how it is going to work. Do you know what I have learned? I have learned that it is none of our business how it's going to work!

I rang up the brother and told him I wanted to buy the car. He told me he needed a £1,000 as a deposit. I had the money so I sent it to him. About eight weeks later, he called to say that the car was ready for delivery and I needed to forward the other £3,000. I said, "That's interesting," because I had no money. Let me explain what "no money" means, because some of you do not understand.

It was not that I hadn't been to the ATM, or that I had investments that I could pull; I had NO money. We were preaching together on the weekend, so I told him that I would bring the money then. I preached every sermon that weekend on faith—for my benefit!

At the end of the weekend, I nervously wrote the cheque without telling him there was nothing in the account. I thought he could enjoy the party. While driving home the devil began to mess with my head.

He told me that what I had done was fraud, and that people go to jail for fraud. At the same time, I reminded Jesus that He had told me to trust Him. But I was a little desperate. I said something like, "If I'm going to jail, You are coming too. You told me to do this."

Without sending out a newsletter or telling anybody, in two weeks God sent exactly £3,000 to me. I banked the money, rang up my friend, and asked if the cheque had bounced. He said that it hadn't and that he had actually had a funny experience with that cheque. He had put it into an inner pocket in his jacket and it had slipped through a hole in the lining. He had lost the cheque for two weeks!

That was a seminal early experience for me in totally trusting Jesus. I learned that I could trust Jesus if I had a definite word from Him. Would I encourage you to write a cheque if you do not have the funds in the bank? Probably not. Is Jesus going to send you thousands of pounds or cause cheques to disappear until the money is there?

It's unlikely. We should test all things. However, this one-time experience taught me that a word from Jesus is trustworthy.

In fact, you can take it to the bank!

Hebrews 11:1 says, *"Faith is the confident assurance that what we hope for is going to happen."* The language of the text is legal in its terminology. Faith will give you the title deed. Imagine those of you with European heritage getting a letter in the post from a German lawyer.

In the letter, it says that you have inherited a castle with 15 bedrooms and 15 bathrooms, and that is just for your pet. There is a three-car garage with a BMW, a Porsche, and a Mercedes. You have never seen the property, never looked at the walnut floors, never seen the colour of those cars, but you have a letter in your hands that says it is all yours. That is what faith is. Faith puts the title deed in your hand that says that it is all yours.

When circumstances are chaotic and everything is breaking out, the title deed says it is going to be all right. It does not matter what the circumstances are or what the devil says. The word of the Lord inside my spirit says it is going to be all right.

Some of you reading this need to understand that it is going to be all right. Even as you are reading, you are mixing what

I am saying with faith and there is a confidence coming inside of you that says, "The circumstances and reports look pretty bad, but what am I going to believe? *If God is for us,* who can be against us?"[8]

This is why you were born.

Join me in praying this prayer out loud at the end of this chapter and the prayers written in several subsequent chapters.

Lord Jesus, I know you are calling me to a life of faith. Increase the faith that I have and let your supernatural actions flow through my life. I receive this in Jesus' name.

What is Faith: Study Guide

Flight Plan

Scripture says that *"Faith shows the reality of what we hope for; it is the evidence of things we cannot see."* (Hebrews 11:1 NLT) What does that really mean? How does it translate into our modern lives now? Have we diminished faith to simply a belief or mental assent vs the active, real-time demonstration of trust in God that faith truly is? In this chapter, Ian unpacked the ingredients of healthy faith which include:

Faith is an Attitude

Faith is an Action

Faith is Obedience

Faith is Agreement

Faith is Assurance

Let's take time to investigate the myths around what faith is and build a solid foundation for faith to grow from in our lives.

Consider this quote:

"There are three definitive conditions for faith to be activated. First, we must know what God has said. Second, we have to be radically obedient to what God has said. Third, we must continue in what God has said."

Take-Off

Growing up you formed a picture of what faith was. How would you describe it? Did it feel tangible and practical or mythical and abstract? So often the best conclusion we can come up with is that faith means to believe. Scripture says in James 2:19 that even the demons believe there is one God and shudder, so faith must mean more. In Hebrew scriptures the word faith is often written as "trust". Read Hebrews 11:1 and 11:6 using the worth trust instead of faith. How does this impact how you interpret these scriptures?

In the opening Chapter Ian recounts a story of having his wallet stolen while travelling by train. He, like us, went through the usual emotions of frustration and anger as he anticipated the implications of what had happened.

A thought, "You have been blessed" danced through his mind. He had a choice – to embrace the truth of that phrase and let faith rise up, or continue to ruminate in his self-pity and defeat.

He chose faith, prayed according to that faith - expressing trust to God in that moment - and he saw his wallet, minus the money, returned to him.

Can you identify any moments in your history where you can see the choice you had in a moment to either embrace faith and trust, or remain in worry and anxious thinking? Share or journal about this moment and allow God to highlight things you may have missed.

Flight Crew

Discussion Questions:

1) Do you see evidence in your past where faith was passive (mental agreement) vs active (taking a risk in trust)?

2) What did you learn in this chapter that helped you better understand faith?

3) What areas in your life do you see faith for "I can't"?

4) What areas do you struggle with faith because you do not have a specific word from God on the matter?

5) Do you believe that we can ask God and hear an answer?

6) What stops you from asking God for a word on the matter?

7) How would you rate your commitment to radical obedience (1 is no commitment, 10 is all in.)?

8) Is there something God has asked of you, that you have not done yet?

9) Do you see any areas in your life where you have made obedience conditional upon understanding the "how" or seeing the end result?

Captain's Log

Reflection: Which of the discussion questions above jumps out at you? What patterns or tendencies do you see in your history in this area? What opportunity is being presented to you for growth and transformation?

Journal prompt: If faith is a demonstration in word, attitude and action that you trust God – is there enough evidence to convict you in your life?

Spend time with Holy Spirit and explore this question honestly. Close your time with God by asking God what your next step of obedience is to take a step in recalibration.

In-Flight Training

In order to move what you have read, reflected on, discussed or journaled from a place of information to a place of transformation you need to act. Just as a pilot will practice for hours using simulations, we need to practice faith in small areas of our life so we can tackle bigger, more complex manoeuvres. Take time to map out an action plan for this week using the following questions:

1) What is one change you want to make? What is your next step of obedience?
2) What actions will you commit to in order to practice this change?
3) How often will you practice?
4) Who will you be accountable to?
5) When will you start?

Checking IN or Checking OUT?

Paul admonishes the Corinthian Church in 2 Corinthians 2:11 to be careful not to let the enemy outsmart us, for we are "are familiar" with his evil schemes.

Change is hard. Faith is important. The enemy does not want you to step into either of them.

Take a moment to listen to your inner dialogue as you consider the commitments you are making. What temptations to "check out" of these commitments do you see? What justification creeps in that allows you not to take this too seriously? What hurry, worry or fear knocks at the door? What power do you have available to you to deal with these enemy tactics? What will you choose when they confront you this week?

Will you check IN or check OUT?

Ground Control

In John 10:27, Jesus describes those who believe as sheep. "My sheep listen to my voice, I know them and they follow me." Jesus is the shepherd; His sheep know His voice. God is our Father and good fathers speak to their children. Discerning how God speaks to us is normal Christian living, in fact we cannot truly live out all that God has for us without it.

Set some time aside for silence and solitude. Invite your heavenly Father to speak to you by His Holy Spirit. What thoughts bubble up? What is the still small voice whispering to you?

1) Write it down.

2) Test it. (Is it congruent with the nature of God and with scripture?)

3) Make it sacred; do not dismiss it, but take it seriously.

Soaring Higher

Who in your life do you see has a life marked by faith? Ask them to tell you their story. Take note of the lessons they learned and the struggles they express. Write down what you learn. What signs in their lives indicated a life of faith? Ask them to pray for you.

Faith is an agreement. An agreement can work both negatively and positively. If you believe you can, you can. If you believe you can't, you can't. Faith will always reach its objective.

Stepping Stones of Faith

For God's sake build not your faith upon Tradition, 'tis as rotten as a rotten Post.[9]

- Nicholas Culpeper, English Scientist

Faith is basic to our Christian lives. The Bible says, *"The righteous will live by faith."*[10] You cannot live the Christian life any other way. G. K. Chesterton said, "The Christian life has not been tried and found wanting, it has been found difficult and left untried." The Christian life is not only difficult, it is impossible. What pleases God is not good thoughts, a new moral standard, or adjusted outward behaviour. There must be a supernatural element in our lives that energises us to live the kind of life that Jesus wants us to live. That element is faith.

The Bible says, "Whatever is not of faith is sin."[11]

Everything we do in our Christian lives needs the element of faith. If it is absent, then our gatherings are nothing more than a Christian club: a community of people who have similar values and believe the same things. However, the Christian community is not a club; it is a community of faith. That is the definitive difference. We have the righteousness of Jesus, not because we read our Bible, say our prayers or pay our tithes. We have been *made righteous* because we placed our trust in Jesus; we expressed our faith. *"This righteousness from God comes through faith in Jesus Christ to all who believe."* [12] Faith operates in a practical way in our lives. I want to share three stepping stones to help you grow in your faith: see something, say something, and then take it.

See Something

Seeing something is the easiest part. Sight, for most of us, is our primary sense. It seems fundamental to our careers, family life, and leisure. Yet, we could be blind to the potential that Jesus has placed in our lives and families. We have to get our perception beyond what we see at this level, beyond the visible.

"By faith [Moses] left Egypt, not fearing the king's anger; he

persevered because he saw him who is invisible."[13] Moses was not deterred by what he could see—Pharaoh's anger—he was inspired by what he could not see. He had somehow gained a vision of God. We must get a higher perspective and see the challenges and the opportunities we face as Jesus sees them.

Say Something

Then we have to say something. That is what I call the "faith word". It is the opportunity to express faith. Until we start verbally committing to our faith, very few of us will move towards what we see. Moses told Pharaoh, *"This is what the LORD, the God of Israel, says: 'Let my people go, so that they may hold a festival to me in the desert."*[14] The word of Moses to Pharaoh matched the conviction in his heart that God had spoken. It took courage for Moses to express his faith when doubt was all around him. The spoken faith word enabled God to partner with Moses and to authenticate his message with signs and wonders.

Take It

The third stepping stone is to take it. The Book of Joshua

offers a great example of these three stepping stones in the person of Caleb. He was one of the spies who first went into the Promised Land, along with Joshua and 10 other men. After their reconnaissance, only two of the 12 saw the opportunity: Caleb and Joshua. The other 10 could only see the problem. Now fast-forward 45 years. Joshua 14 records Caleb as saying: *"I was forty years old when Moses the servant of the LORD sent me from Kadesh Barnea to explore the land. And I brought him back a report according to my convictions, but my brothers who went up with me made the hearts of the people melt with fear. I, however, followed the LORD my God wholeheartedly. So on that day Moses swore to me, 'The land on which your feet have walked will be your inheritance and that of your children forever, because you have followed the LORD my God wholeheartedly.' Now then, just as the LORD promised, he has kept me alive for forty-five years since the time he said this to Moses, while Israel moved about in the desert. So here I am today, eighty-five years old! I am still as strong today as the day Moses sent me out; I'm just as vigorous to go out to battle now as I was then. Now give me this hill country that the LORD promised me that day."* [15]

Caleb had a vision that was constant and consistent. After more than 40 years of languishing in the desert, he still envisioned taking the land. Sometimes we have a vision that is great for three weeks, or two years, but we give up on it. However, when vision is so strong that it resonates within us regardless of what life throws at us, the vision remains constant. Caleb said, *"I was 40 years old when Moses, the servant of the Lord, sent me from Kadesh Barnea to explore the land."* That was the **seeing stage**; he went in to reconnoitre the land. To see something, we have to explore the land, check out the opportunities, do some research or draw some comparisons.

One of the things that we are very keen on is our family. When Judith or I see parents that have fantastic teenagers, we want to know how they did it because we have a 19-year-old who is going on 2. To explore the possibilities, you have to get out of your own little world. You have to enter other peoples' worlds to find out how they are doing it or making it happen.

Caleb had gone into the land 45 years previously. When he returned, he *"brought back word to him as it was in my heart."*[16] In fact, each of the spies reported what was in their heart. Caleb and Joshua said, *"We should go in and take the land, for we can certainly do it."*[17] The other 10 spies, however, were so negative that fear melted the hearts of the people.

Caleb's vision of taking the land was put on hold for more than four decades, but the day finally came. Caleb said, "Now give me this hill country that the LORD promised me that day. You yourself heard then that the Anakites were there and their cities were large and fortified, but, the LORD helping me, I will drive them out just as he said."[18] This was the **saying stage.**

Caleb was determined to seize what he saw. I love that verse: *"But the Lord helping me, I will drive them out just as he said."* Sometimes we are nervous to go forward with the picture we have in our mind. We look at our own skill set, our own resource base, our personality and think, "I can't do it." And we would be right. It is with the Lord's help that we do it. We are not pulling it off by ourselves; it is only with the Lord's enabling that we can succeed. The Lord's help turns up in all kinds of different ways. Seize your opportunities. This is the **taking stage.**

Characteristics of Faith

Moses demonstrates characteristics of faith. "By faith, when he had grown up, he refused to be known as the son of Pharaoh's daughter. He chose to be mistreated along with the people of God rather than to enjoy the pleasures of sin for a short time."[19] Moses regarded disgrace for the sake of the LORD as of greater value than the treasures of Egypt because he was looking ahead to his reward. "By faith he left Egypt, not fearing the king's anger, he persevered because he saw him who was invisible."[20] Moses was a great "see it" person: a visionary and a great leader. When we can clarify what we see, that gives incredible power to move forward. When there is lack of clarity, we tend to hedge our bets and often retreat to Plan B.

What do you see for your family, your ministry, and your life? When you see it, and see it clearly, it becomes a mandate for your life. Moses had a clear vision of the next step.

He was not threatened by what he could see: the king's doubt and anger. His mandate came from what he could not see: the vision God had for his life.

Clarity

First of all, clear vision allowed Moses to make difficult decisions. If your vision is fuzzy and has multiple angles to it, then you will get to the point where you will say, "I don't know if I want to make that hard decision. I don't know if this is actually worth it." Moses, however, had a mandate to lead the people of God out of Egypt. It was so clear and succinct that it freed him to make difficult decisions. The toughest decision he made was refusing to be known as the son of Pharaoh's daughter.

That was huge. He had belonged to the royal household. He was Pharaoh's grandson. This was his identity and his pension fund. He was Mr. Giorgio Armani and Mr. Hugo Boss in the community.

Yet, he was able to turn his back on the pedigree and the perks, because the vision was clear. To make difficult decisions you have to have clarity. The cause or the vision for our lives has to be so strong that we are prepared to say no to the things that would prevent us from fulfilling our destiny.

Commitment

Secondly, Moses was willing to pay a high price. The price was to endure ill treatment with the people of God rather than to enjoy the passionate pleasure of sin for a short time. He decided that low-level living was not good enough. Rather than watching four hours of TV every night, it will mean spending an hour a night on personal development. "Oh my gosh, the Olympic Games are on!"

"I've got to watch Game of Thrones to see if Lannister will pay his debts." When you have clarity, you are prepared to pay a high price. Though the price seems high now, it will seem economical six months from now.

When the picture is clear, you are willing to make the sacrifice because you realise the value.

The Long View

Thirdly, faith allowed Moses to focus on an eternal rather than a temporal goal. Let me ask you a question: what are you living for? Some people are living for a paycheque, others for retirement, and others for a secure pension. But, retirement to what? For what reason? There are people in their 20s who could create a financial plan so that by the time they are 45 or 50, they could be financially free to serve Jesus without having to raise missions support. You could then spend the next 25 or 30 years in "full-time Christian service." You could, if you have a vision for it. It is easy to be driven by the mundane, temporal, hassling, irritating stuff of life. That stuff can drive the vision out of our minds. Friends, we are involved in an eternal plan.

It is not about surviving until the end of the week, or paying off the mortgage or getting to retirement. All these things are important in themselves, but there is something greater. We have to see the context into which the temporal fits into God's eternal plan. When we have clarity regarding the long-range view, we can confidently commit to making the decisions that will bring it about.

No Fear

The fourth benefit of faith is it helps overcome fear in life. By faith, Moses entered Egypt, *not fearing* the wrath of the king. Have you ever seen people do things you thought were extraordinary, or outrageous or risky and said to yourself, "Man, I couldn't have done that!" Someone once said to me, "I don't know if I could do what all the people at NLI have been doing: moving to a new country, living by faith, and raising missions support."

Well, the reality is, when you have a clear picture of God's plan the fear is nowhere near as great, because you have faith that it is the right thing to do.

Are there things percolating in your life that have been there for a very long time and for any number of reasons you have not been able to push forward? Get absolute clarity, commit yourself to God's long-term plan and you will find the courage to seize your future in Jesus' name.

What if it Sounds Stupid?

Hebrews 11:13 says, "All these people were still living by faith when they died. They did not receive the things promised. They only saw them and welcomed them from a distance and admitted they were aliens and strangers on the earth." There are steps we need to take to stay in our vision. The moment we start speaking our vision it moves from the private and personal, to the public and corporate. Sometimes we are nervous to share what is in our hearts; after all, what if it sounds stupid. Well, let us find out! Why secretly hold on to something stupid? Why not bring some collective wisdom to our stupidity? We do not have all the resources to bring vision to fruition, whether it is for business, church, life or children. God has designed it like this. We need other people in our lives to make us the person that we need to be.

When we put our vision on the table, it gives others the opportunity to add something, to spot a flaw, or to affirm it. That provides faith and fuel to go forward.

Too often, we are too conscious of saving face. "If we let it out of the bag then everybody will know about it, and what if it does not work?" Hey, if it does not work, it does not work! What is wrong with that? Life is an experiment; it is not about winning and losing. In fact, if you can change the word *failure* to

experiment, you will find yourself liberated.

"I am just going to experiment with some things." Thomas Edison, the inventor of the light bulb insisted that he had not initially failed – he had learned the value of finding 10,000 ways that wouldn't work. The benefit of experimenting is finding out how to do and how *not* to do things. We will begin to speak our faith, and express a level of confidence in what we believe. *"I have believed,"* the Bible says, *"and therefore I have spoken."*[21] The moment we say something, we are committed to what we have said. Of course, that is often why we say nothing. It is imperative to throw the vision on the table for your life, your ministry, your family, your marriage or your business.

It Sounds Like Jesus

When Jesus asks us to do something, it is normally too big

for us. If we think we can manage it, take it as a word from the devil. If we cannot manage it, it is probably Jesus, because Jesus loves to stretch us. Jesus sees so much more potential in us than we see in ourselves. As we articulate the vision, Jesus brings people along to participate in the vision. We will find that the vision gains energy and life. People give us the legs to move the vision forward. Clear conviction follows. After we have spoken a faith word, it is amazing what happens: we start believing what we are saying. After we have articulated the vision and other people have helped shaped it, we get clear conviction.

Seize the Day

Finally, it's time to seize the day—to put faith into action. Some Israelites got to the edge of the river but never crossed in to the Promised Land. Faith requires new levels of courage and discipline. Sometimes we do not know the difference between being concerned and being committed. Here are six keys to securing the dream.

1) State the dream. After you read this chapter, I would encourage you to take a piece of paper and write down your dream. Do it in multiple areas—personal,

family, career, finances and ministry. Before you can follow the dream, you have to articulate it.

2) Examine your motives. Ask yourself, "Why do I want that?" This will help you to sift your motivation to ensure it is for God's glory not self-aggrandisement.

3) Consider the options. I wonder how many different ways there are of reaching your goals? There are about 50 different ways to drive to Manchester, but I normally go the same way. Often times, we think there is only one way to achieve our vision, but there are 50 or a 100 different ways. If we keep our goals to ourselves, we limit our options. However, the moment they are out on the table the options multiply, and suddenly there is fuel and energy coming into our lives.

4) Utilise resources. You already have financial, experiential, intellectual, spiritual, and entrepreneurial resources. What you do not yet have is going to come. That is why it is called a walk of faith. Resources follow faith; they do not precede it. Verbalising faith and vision creates the opportunity for resources to materialise.

5) Remove non-essentials. Do not begin with a Rolls Royce vision. Keep to the essentials.

6) Embrace the challenges. It may look scary, it may look

large, it may look beyond us, but approach it like eating an elephant: one bite at a time. Embrace the opportunity. Move to your God-given potential one step at a time, one conversation, one prayer, one agreement, and one good idea at a time. This is how you move toward what Jesus has for you.

Father, thank You for Your Word. Thank You for the power of Your Word and the truth of Your Word. We pray, Lord Jesus, that You would cause Your Word to remain in us. We pray that the enemy would not steal the Word from our lives. We pray for those who face incredible obstacles and opportunities. We pray that faith would come into their hearts to have confidence that it is going to be alright—better than alright. We pray for those who are thinking of the kind of family they want to build and for their children to reach their full potential. We pray for those who live on their own. We pray there would be connections within the Body of Christ to fan the flame of their destiny and purpose. Lord, we pray that faith and fire would rise up inside of us so that we will not take life as it is dished out to us. Instead, help us to take life and seize it with both hands to establish your kingdom in our generation. Amen!

Stepping Stones of Faith:

Study Guide

Flight Plan

We know that God has given each of us a measure of faith (Romans 12: 3). 2 Thessalonians 1:3 suggests that our faith can grow more and more. So how do we grow in our faith? The stepping stones to faith are simple, but perhaps not always easy:

1) See Something – Higher Perspective – Seeing What Jesus Sees
2) Say Something – Express your faith in words
3) Take It – Persist until you obtain it
4) Characteristics of Faith:
    a. Clarity
    b. Commitment
    c. Long View

      d. No Fear

5) Check my Pride

Take note what comes to mind when we reread these statements:

"Until we start verbally committing to our faith, very few of us will move towards what we see

"Faith requires new levels of courage and discipline."

Take-Off

In this chapter we looked to the life of Moses as an example of living by faith. There were four characteristics in Moses that are good clues to us about what it will take to be a person of faith.

1) Clarity: Moses was a man of vision

2) Commitment: Moses was willing to pay a high price

3) Long View: Moses chose to focus on the eternal rather than the temporal.

4) No Fear: Moses did not let fear stop him from obedience.

The cycle that connects these four characteristics is also important to note. Without clarity, we begin to doubt and have less reason to sacrifice or commit. Without commitment it is impossible to see the long view, because we are already looking for an exit strategy. Without the long view, it is much more difficult to overcome fear because we have not put ourselves in the place of victory that is already purchased for us.

Lastly, fear robs us of clarity, and the rut deepens. Jesus, for the joy set before him, endured the cross, scorning its shame. Like Moses, Jesus was crystal clear about His job. He was willing to pay whatever price to see it done. The view of eternal joy was his motivation and death itself could not stop him. Can you see a connection between small faith and lack of clarity in what God has asked of you?

Flight Crew

Discussion Questions:

1) Have you seen examples in your own History with God where clarity on what God has said helped you follow through?

   a. If yes – Share

   b. If No - how can you pursue greater clarity?

2) In what situations in your life/history has faith for the negative (I can't, did God really say?) robbed you of taking

next steps?

3) Where can you see temporal goals at play in your life over eternal ones?

4) Is there an area right now that God is highlighting to you? Where are you on this journey?

    a. See

    b. Say

    c. Seize

5) How do you feel about experimenting in your journey of faith?

    a. Where does the need to do it perfectly (Success & Failure) rob you from experimenting?

    b. What is at the root of the fear of getting it wrong for you?

    c. Where does pride play a role in this for you?

    d. Where do you see hesitancy to commit?

Captain's Log

Reflection: Review the 6 keys outlined in the Seize the Day section on pages 81-83. What is an area in your life that God is highlighting right now?

Journal Prompts: Go through the 6 keys in your journal around this area God has highlighted and see what clarity God brings you.

In-Flight Training

What is your next step in faith forward? Ask Holy Spirit now to give you a step of obedience to take.

1) What did He ask you to do? (Write down the specific directions.)

2) When will you start experimenting?

3) Who will you invite to this journey of faith with you as accountability and support?

4) When will you start?

Checking IN or Checking OUT?

Take a moment to listen to your inner dialogue as you consider the commitments you are making. What temptations to "check out" of these commitments do you see? What justification creeps in that allows you not to take this too seriously? What hurry, worry or fear knocks at the door? What power do you have available to you to deal with these enemy tactics? What will you choose when they confront you this week?

Will you check IN or check OUT?

Ground Control

Set some time aside for silence and solitude. Invite your heavenly Father to speak to you by His Holy Spirit. What thoughts bubble up? What is the still small voice whispering to you?

1) Write it down.

2) Test it. (Is it congruent with the nature of God and with scripture?)

3) Make it sacred; do not dismiss it, but take it seriously.

Soaring Higher

There are several examples of See, Say, Seize in scripture. Take a look at these other examples and identify the See, Say and Seize in each one. What insights are applicable in your life right now?

1) Jehoshaphat - 2 Chronicles 20

2) Elisha – 2 Kings 6

3) Paul & Silas – Acts 16

Faith requires new levels of courage and discipline.

Doubting the Doubt

"Every mental act is composed of doubt and belief, but it is belief that is the positive, it is belief that sustains thought and holds the world together."[22]

— Søren Kierkegaard

"Now Thomas (called Didymus), one of the Twelve, was not with the disciples when Jesus came. So the other disciples told him, "We have seen the Lord!" But he said to them, "Unless I see the nail marks in his hands and put my finger where the nails were, and put my hand into his side, I will not believe it." A week later his disciples were in the house again, and Thomas was with them. Though the doors were locked, Jesus came and stood among them and said, "Peace be with you!" Then he said to Thomas, "Put your finger here; see my hands. Reach out your hand and put it into my side. Stop doubting and believe."

Thomas said to him, "My Lord and my God!" Then Jesus told him, "Because you have seen me, you have believed; blessed are those who have not seen and yet have believed."

Jesus did many other miraculous signs in the presence of his disciples, which are not recorded in this book. But these are written that you may believe that Jesus is the Christ, the Son of God, and that by believing you may have life in his name" (John 20:24-31[NIV]).

Consider this phrase, *"Stop doubting and believe."* Christianity is based upon faith. Christianity is not a religion or some kind of sect with rules and routines. Rather, it is faith in the living person of Jesus Christ. This is the fundamental difference between Christianity and other belief systems and religions to which people are attached. Faith in the living Son of God is critical to experiencing all that God has for us.

As Christians, we are challenged in our faith the same way the Apostle Thomas was challenged.

Often, we experience a crisis of faith after we first come to Jesus. We have questions to ask, doubts to express and certainty to find. For me it took five months of discussing, arguing, debating, shouting, and trying to make my point. Eventually, I was overwhelmed with the reality of Jesus' death on the cross and His resurrection from the dead. I had to respond to that and put my faith in Christ. This is the crisis of faith that we can have when we first come to Christ.

The Roots of Doubt

To experience what the scripture calls *"life in His name,"*[23] there must be a continual activation of our faith to receive all that God has for us. The Bible says this, "The just shall live by a bit of luck." NO, it says, *"The just shall live by faith"*[24]; faith in the Son of God. Thomas's challenge to believe came at a very unfortunate time. He was out of fellowship with Jesus.

This was the third or fourth resurrection appearance of Christ, and Thomas had not been around any of the times that Jesus had appeared. He found it very difficult when challenged to believe.

Out of Fellowship with Jesus

It is always difficult to respond to the challenge of faith if we are out of fellowship with Jesus. The reason for this is that our faith response is not just a mental thing. Faith operates out of a relationship with Christ; it is more than a theological understanding of who Christ is. Have you noticed that many of life's greatest challenges do *not* happen after a Sunday morning service when we are really pumped up? They usually come at the most inconvenient time. Challenges rarely come when we are prepared and our spiritual lives are in order.

Out of Synch with Believers

It is difficult to have faith for anything when we are out of fellowship with Jesus. The disciples testified to Thomas, "Hey Thomas, we have seen the Lord." He replied, "Get on your bike, baby. What are you talking about? How can you have seen the Lord? He is dead!" (The Green paraphrase). When we are out of relationship with Jesus, we find it difficult to receive encouragement, counsel, or even words of faith from other Christians. We find it difficult to get on board, not because we think they are liars, but because our connection is weak.

Like Thomas, we are often getting spiritual encouragement or insights second-hand and find them hard to believe.

Out of Line with Scripture

Once we begin to doubt what other believers tell us, we start making the Bible say what we want it to say. Thomas said, "I will not believe." We do not believe with our *wills*. The Bible says that we believe with our heart and confess with our mouth. However, when we are out of connection with Jesus and start disbelieving what others are saying about the Lord, we tend to manipulate the scriptures.

Out of Touch with Jesus

Next, we can even begin to reject what Jesus says. Thomas knew that Jesus has prophesied, "Destroy this temple, and in three days I will build it again.[25] ...but the only sign I will give them is the sign of the prophet Jonah. For as Jonah was in the belly of the great fish for three days and three nights, so will the Son of Man be in the heart of the earth for three days and three nights."[26] When we are out of connection with Jesus, we start disbelieving the testimony of Scripture and doubt the Word of God. In this walk of faith, we often want to understand the beginning from the end.

We want to understand it all. But God says, "I want you to

trust Me. You want to understand; I want you to trust. You want to feel good; I want you to live right. You want to be blessed; I want you holy." There comes a time when we have to surrender to the Lordship of Jesus and get reconnected. Then, the flow of encouragement can come from the Body, the scriptures can come alive, and the words of Christ can be re-established as the basis for living.

The interesting thing about this story is what transpired after the challenge came to Thomas to *"Stop doubting and believe."* Jesus went on to say, *"Blessed are those that have believed and have not seen."* First Corinthians 15:5-7 catalogues the people who saw Jesus with their own eyes after the resurrection: Peter, The Twelve, the 500, James, all the apostles and Paul. However, there are billions of other people, like you and me, who have not seen Jesus with our physical eyes, yet have believed. When we heard the good news, faith welled up inside of us enabling us to believe that Jesus died for our sins. We believe Jesus has the power of an endless life and that His endless life lives inside of us.

Hebrews 11 lists a whole gang of people that believed yet had no physical evidence. There is Noah. His life is a great story, but if you had actually had to live it out, it would have been a pretty challenging deal. The Lord said, "I want you to build a boat." Noah had never heard the word *boat* before. Noah must have wondered, "Now, why on earth would we need a honking big boat like that?" And the Lord replied, "Because it is going to *rain*. In fact, Noah, I am going to flood the earth." That would have been another new word, because up until then, the earth had not experienced rain.

Noah no doubt wondered, "Boat, rain and flood…what's going on here?" He began to cut down trees, hack out planks, and buy some nails. All his mates were saying, "What's going on, Noah?" "Oh, I'm building a boat." "Why are you building a boat?" "Oh, it's going to rain." "Going to *what*?" For the next 100 years, while building this honking big boat, his mates reminded him, "It ain't raining yet, Noah. Did you get the word wrong?" It is a story of persevering faith. And of course, the boat came in handy when it did rain.

Think of Moses. God said, "Mo, go through the Red Sea. Put that stick over the sea and something will happen." Could Moses have been thinking, "But God, I have about three million people behind me and they are just a little agitated at the moment because we've got a bunch of Egyptians after us and they want to make us into Jewish hamburgers. And what happens if the stick breaks before it hits the water?" These are great stories until you have to live them.

Inside of You

The resurrection of Jesus reminds us that we were born to be a miraculous people. We were never meant to live on a normal level or just survive; the resurrection power of the Son of God is inside of us. It is the power of the indestructible person of the Lord Jesus Christ, who said, *"Let there be light,"* and 93 million miles away the sun appeared. That power resides in us by the power of the resurrection.

The Bible says, "Anyone who wants to come to him must believe that God exists and that he rewards those who sincerely seek him."[27] What Noah and Moses did, and what Thomas was about to do, are going to be normal for us. When I preach this, I tell people that we can supply them with nappies at the end of the message. But this is where we have to move to. For our North American readers, nappies are not the sleep you have during a church service. A nappy is the Queen's proper English for what those from the new world call a "diaper". Unless we are doing the impossible, believing for the ridiculous, we are not normal. We are designed to have a supernatural, resurrection stamp on our lives.

Faith that comes by seeing is good, but faith that comes by hearing is better. *"The just shall live by faith."* We walk by faith, we live by faith, we give by faith, and we witness by faith. It all comes by faith!

Four Errors

Thomas made four critical errors. When he was challenged to believe, he did *not* **reject the negative lies.** His closest friends told him they had seen Jesus. He said, *"Unless I see...."* He was telling them and telling himself that what they were saying could not be true. It was impossible. When somebody says to us, "It can be done; It is true," we have to learn to reject the negative lie in our mind that tells us the opposite.

The second thing Thomas did *not* do was **respond to truth positively.** He said, *"I will not believe."* We will find it difficult to act on a particular truth until we begin to operate in general truth. For example, unless we start at a general truth like, *"... with God all things are possible,"*[28] then when we are going to find it difficult to believe anything detailed or precise. If we do not start to believe the general revelation of Scripture, it will be difficult to have faith for a miracle.

The third thing Thomas did *not* do was **rely upon Christ implicitly**. It is not a doctrine that we are confessing; it is Christ we are confessing. When everything around us says, "there is no hope", we have to trust Jesus.

When we tell our self, "You are going to look like a flipping idiot," we have to trust Jesus. Jesus had told his disciples, "The Son of Man must suffer many things and be rejected by the elders, chief priests and teachers of the law, and that he must be killed and after three days rise again."[29] Thomas should have remembered that; even the chief priests and the Pharisees—the unbelievers—remembered it.[30] And if Thomas remembered it, he did not believe it. We should trust the word of Jesus.

The last thing Thomas did *not* do was **bow down in worship**. It was not until Thomas touched the nail scarred hands and felt the wounded torso of Jesus that he believed. *"Blessed are those who have not seen and yet have believed."* After we have rejected the negative lies, responded to truth, relied upon Jesus, we must close the back door of unbelief. We do this by confessing the glory and power of the Lord. He has more than enough power to do what we are asking Him to do. Jesus is the Author and Finisher of our faith.

Whatever our challenge is right now, we have to get the Word, we have to respond to the Word, and we have to hold fast to the Word. We cannot give a single inch on the Word.

Faith is Not Denial

Romans 4 tells us to face the facts. It was utterly impossible for Abraham and Sarah to have children. Abraham was 100 years young and Sarah was 90. It was hopeless. The Bible uses great graphic language to describe their physical potential for conceiving a child: *"his body was as good as dead... and Sarah's womb was dead."*[31] In human terms, a son and heir were impossible. Faith is not denying the facts. Some people deny obvious illness, others pretend their financial difficulties do not exist, while others overlook dire circumstances. They have gotten this whacky idea that denying the facts is an expression of faith.

Abraham accepted the facts: he and Sarah were both past it. Romans 4:18 says, *"Against all hope, Abraham in hope believed and so became the father of many nations."* What did he believe? He believed the promise that God had given him 25 years before: "A son coming from your own body will be your heir."[32]

When we are in a crisis of faith, we have to be real. We cannot pretend, "It is not that bad." We will not increase our faith by minimising the difficulty. No, we have to say, "This is bad, stinking bad. God, I need a miracle or we are in a mess." That is where Abraham and Sarah were—against all hope. They looked at the paperwork, they looked at each other but did not lose hope.

Verse 19 says, *"Without weakening in his faith, he faced the fact."* You can look the facts in the eye without losing faith. They faced the facts. Verse 21 says, *"He did not waver through unbelief regarding the promise of God, but was strengthened in his faith and gave glory to God."*

How do we keep faith constant during a crisis of faith? Abraham did not waver in his faith because he held on to the promise of God. He was fully persuaded that God had power to do what He had promised. We can keep our faith from wavering by declaring who God is and what God is. Declare His covenant names. Praise Him as the Living God, the Almighty God, the Creator, the Sustainer, and the Divine Source of all things. Remember past victories and trust in Him regardless of the problem. We affirm faith in our spirit by confessing the Word, the work, and the character of God with our lips. This does something in our heart that causes faith to solidify so that we can stand resolute in our faith.

There are only two kinds of Christians: those who doubt and those who believe. There are two kinds of covenant: that of the flesh and that of the Spirit. The Christian life is based on faith, and the thing that activates faith is trusting in the risen Son of God. We have choices to make.

When we are sick and we are prayed for and anointed with oil, we can end up with a greasy head or mix the anointing with faith and receive the healing touch of Jesus Christ. When we take the bread and wine of holy communion, by faith we receive the broken body and the blood of the Lord Jesus Christ. When the offering plate goes by us and we put our money in, we can either pay a debt or sow a seed. It is the resurrection life of Jesus that energises the faith that is already there so we can get back to normal Biblical Christianity. The Lord says to us, like He said to Thomas, *"Stop doubting and believe.*

Father, I want to believe You instead of following doubts or fears. I thank You that Your strength, hope and faith are rising in me to trust You more. Please help me, Father, to doubt the doubt and trust You instead of trusting doubt. I thank you that all of the seeds of scripture I have heard and studied are producing a harvest of faith now; that faith has come by hearing and hearing by the Word of God. I receive it in Jesus' name, Amen!

Doubting the Doubt: Study Guide

Flight Plan

Doubt is a complex and ever-present reality in our lives but often we justify its presence or even go so far as to welcome it with open arms in efforts not to be narrow-minded. In this chapter Ian challenged us to doubt the doubt and gave us clues to circumstances that can actually open the door to faith-robbing doubt. He explored four significant roots of doubt in our lives:

1) Out of Fellowship with Jesus
2) Out of Sync with Believers
3) Out of Line with Scripture
4) Out of Touch with Jesus

As you read this chapter, which one of these jumped out at you? What questions do you still have about doubt and how to deal with it in your life? Who can you talk to about it? Will you?

Take-Off

Let's imagine for a moment that you are nearing retirement and while you were praying this morning in your devotions God began to speak to you about the specifics of an invention He wanted you to make. He wants you to design an air purification system for buildings that takes radiation out of the air and replaces it with oxygen. For the world you cannot see how this tech would be needed in our current world, and you are pretty sure you aren't going to live long enough to see life on Mars. You can't shake it though, the instructions are clear, and specific. After 5 years, 10 years, 25 years of working on this project, spending your money, and having your time and life consumed by this project your best friend sits you down and confronts your "wild fantasies."

- "The problem you are trying to solve, doesn't even exist!"
- "Why are you wasting so much time and resource?"
- "Did God really say?"
- "If this was really God, he would have said…"
- "You aren't stewarding your resources in a Godly way!"

These are the doubts your friend is having but surely there

would also be a host of personal doubts you could add to the pile.

This is a reality Noah must have experienced. He was building a boat, miles away from any bodies of water, for a problem that didn't exist (It had likely never rained to that point, like the garden of Eden the ground was watered from beneath.) He started this journey well into his life and the project took 100+ years to complete. That is a long commitment to an idea that doesn't make rational sense. Putting yourself in his shoes as best you can, what doubts would you have wrestled with?

Flight Crew

Discussion Questions:

1) In Noah's case, what role did relationship with God play in His ability to sustain such a singular, long, difficult road of obedience?

2) Why do we think our relationship with God is any less significant than it was for Noah?

3) So often God speaks to us, we disregard or dismiss what He says and only until it comes out of someone else's mouth do we reconsider its validity. Have you ever experienced this? Why do we do this?

4) Ian said: "Unless we are doing the impossible and believing for the ridiculous, we are not normal." What goes through your head when you hear this?

   a. What rational/mental objections bubble up?

   b. How does your spirit respond?

   c. Can you sense the difference between the two – likely simultaneous responses? (Spirit and soul/ mind) Explore this.

      i. How much space or time do you need to hold this tension to get to a place of mindful choosing?

5) In what areas of your life to you recognise the tension between walking/talking in faith and denying what is really happening? What have you learned in this chapter about navigating this?

Captain's Log

Reflection: Reread pages 94-96– Reflect on where you see these 4 errors in your own journey and history. What is Holy Spirit highlighting for you?

Journal Prompts: Take a day to explore each of these errors this week. Reread the section of the book and the journal your response.

> **Journal: Day 1** Reject the Negative Lies
>
> **Journal: Day 2** Respond to Truth Positively
>
> **Journal: Day 3** Rely upon Christ Implicitly
>
> **Journal: Day 4** Bow Down in Worship

In-Flight Training

What is your next step in faith forward? What disciplines do you need? Ask Holy Spirit now to give you a step of obedience to take.

1) What did He ask you to do? (Write down the specific directions.)
2) When will you start experimenting?
3) Who will you invite to this journey of faith with you as accountability and support?
4) When will you start?

Checking IN or Checking OUT?

Take a moment to listen to your inner dialogue as you consider the commitments you are making. What temptations to "check out" of these commitments do you see? What justification creeps in that allows you not to take this too seriously? What hurry, worry or fear knocks at the door?

What power do you have available to you to deal with these enemy tactics? What will you choose when they confront you this week?

Will you check IN or check OUT?

Ground Control

Set some time aside for silence and solitude. Invite your heavenly Father to speak to you by His Holy Spirit. What thoughts bubble up? What is the still small voice whispering to you?

1) Write it down.
2) Test it. (Is it congruent with the nature of God and with scripture?)
3) Make it sacred; do not dismiss it, but take it seriously.

Soaring Higher

Commit to building a new discipline for 30 days, journal what you learn.

Unless we are doing the impossible and believing for the ridiculous, we are not normal.

Ever-Increasing Faith

Faith is not something to grasp, it is a state to grow into.[33]

- Mahatma Gandhi

"Yet it was good of you to share in my troubles. Moreover, as you Philippians know, in the early days of your acquaintance with the gospel, when I set out from Macedonia, not one church shared with me in the matter of giving and receiving, except you only; for even when I was in Thessalonica, you sent me aid again and again when I was in need. Not that I am looking for a gift, but I am looking for what may be credited to your account. I have received full payment and even more; I am amply supplied, now that I have received from Epaphroditus the gifts you sent. They are a fragrant offering, an acceptable sacrifice, pleasing to God. And my God will meet all your needs according to his glorious riches in Christ Jesus. To our God and Father be glory for ever and ever. Amen."[34]

If you have been in church any amount of time, you will have probably heard verse 19 of that passage quoted: *"My God shall supply all of my needs according to His glorious riches in Christ Jesus."* It is an incredible verse; it is a verse filled with potency. The only difficulty with the verse is… it doesn't work.

The Bible says that God will meet all of our needs according to His glorious riches in Christ Jesus, but it doesn't work. Individuals have needs. Churches and mission organisations are jam-packed with needs. So, the verse doesn't work. I can see only two ways of dealing with this problem. First, get the scissors and cut this little verse out of your Bible. You will feel a lot better. Or secondly, try to understand why it doesn't work. Perhaps we should try the second option before we start cutting up the New Testament.

The problem begins here. It is difficult to claim verse 19 unless we are actually living verses 14-18. This verse can only work when we actually put the verses prior to it into action. The Bible says that the Philippian church had been kind, loving, and generous in the matter of giving and receiving. They had helped advance the gospel in many different ways.

Because of their generosity to Paul and to others, God would generously meet their needs. This is not a *sticky plaster* verse – or as they say in Canada, a "Band-Aid". We have not properly applied verses 14-18.

Generosity

The premise is this: I must be generous to other people. Proverbs 11:25 says, *"A generous man will prosper and he who refreshes others will himself be refreshed."* Jesus said that if you give to others, God will give back to you.[35] If we want to invoke God's blessing upon our lives, then we have to adopt a generous lifestyle. My giving and your giving become an encouragement to people.

One of the results of becoming a generous person is that *you have a life that is much bigger than your own.* Even though we are missionaries ourselves, as a family, we support eight other missionaries. We send money every month to a couple from our church who are helping the deaf community in Uganda. We send money because money is a representation of our life. I give up time and energy to get money. When I give money to them, I am actually sending a part of my life on a monthly basis.

Every month I am in Uganda, helping deaf people to communicate, plus giving them an opportunity to experience the love of Jesus, even though I have never been to Uganda!

We support a woman working in the heart of Belfast. I have not been in Belfast for many years, but every month my money is in Belfast going into her account. When you make a financial commitment to missions, you end up with a much bigger life.

My giving becomes an encouragement to other people.

An Investment

Verse 17 says my giving is an investment for the future. Paul reminds the Philippians: *Though I appreciate the gifts, what makes me happy is the well-earned reward you have because of your kindness* (my paraphrase). In the original language, the phrase *well-earned reward* means "accumulated interest." Have you ever experienced accumulated interest on a credit card? It is not encouraging. Perhaps you receive accumulated interest on your investments. That is encouraging. The Bible says that God wants us to accumulate interest in our lives. The Bible says that those who have left homes and families for the cause of the gospel shall in this life receive a hundred times as much and inherit eternal life.[36] Do you know how much that is? That is 10,000 per cent! I want 10,000 per cent. Do you? Every time I am investing into the propagation of the gospel, I'm accumulating in my heavenly bank account a resource base that, from time to time, I can draw on to further advance the gospel yet again. Paul wrote, *"Give happily to those in need and always be ready to share whatever God has given you. By doing this, you will be storing up real treasure for yourselves in heaven, it is the only safe investment for eternity."*[37]

The story is told of two guys, John and Wayne, who died and went to heaven. They served in the same church, were friends all of their lives and died within moments of each other. When John arrived in heaven, Peter said, "John, it is great to see you! Come and see your heavenly home." John is directed down a golden street to something that looks like a dog's kennel. He was expecting a mansion, but at least he is in heaven. Meanwhile, Wayne is led down a different street to an incredible, palatial mansion. John sheepishly followed along but when he saw Wayne's mansion he blurted out, "Peter, what is going on here?

He has got this big honking thing, and I have got a shed." Peter said, "It is very simple, John. We could only build with what you sent up and you sent up so little."

Some people think they are building up their heavenly bank account because they pay their tithes. We have to remember we do not give tithes, we *pay* tithes. Tithes are rent for living on planet Earth. Remember, we are drinking God's water, eating His food, and breathing His air. For that, all He requires is 10 per cent of our income. Thank you very much.

I know a lot of people love a good deal. God could have said, "I'll take 90 per cent, you keep 10 per cent." But He didn't. So giving only 10 per cent is a pretty good deal, eh?

Just a thought.

A Sacrifice

Verse 18 says giving is *a sacrifice to God*. Paul pointed out that the gift he had received through Epaphroditus was a fragrant offering, an acceptable sacrifice, and pleasing to God. He is referring to the five offerings in Leviticus chapter 7. I do not know if you have met sacrificial people, but there is an aromatic joy that emanates from their lives. It is like expensive perfume. They just love to give—time, resources, and hospitality. They are almost addicted to giving.

There are seasons in our lives when we have to do what the Philippians did. It is important to understand that Philippi was a very poor church. The economics of that city were severe. Yet the Bible says they gave repeatedly to advance the kingdom of God.

I have been to cities like that. In Estonia, one city had an unemployment rate of 62 per cent. I was there to launch a plan to build a large number of churches by 2010. I said to the Estonian leadership, "We've got to get Estonian people to buy into this financially as well as practically." In one meeting, there were about 300 people in the room. I shared my heart about now being the time to rise up and do what needed to be done.

I knew I was speaking to some who were unemployed. I encouraged them to give until there was blood on their hands; that is to give a *sacrificial* offering. Later in the meeting, the offering came to €13,000 (euros), six mobile phones, four wedding rings, eight watches, and two ties. I would like to suggest to you that there was a bit of blood on their hands. They actually saw their personal economic situations of lower importance than the needs of lost people coming to Jesus.

Increase Your Giving

If you are not a giver, start giving today. If you are a giver, increase your giving. If you cannot afford it, sell something so that you can afford it. Is there something that you have been saving for? Perhaps this is the year for you to give it to see lost people come to Jesus. When we give until it hurts, we are opening ourselves to receiving the potential resources of God to meet us in the time of need and famine.

The Source

The **premise** is that I have to be generous. The **promise** is, *"My God shall supply all your needs according to His glorious riches in Christ Jesus."* The source is God. If you think your source is your employer, you have a pretty small resource. When you understand that God is your resource, incredible things begin to happen. You begin to see life through an abundance mentality. There is no limitation with God. If you are categorically, intentionally predetermined to give money away, God can pour resources through your life. But you open the doors in your life for money to flow in by being generous.

Sometimes resources are not flowing in because we are

not letting enough flow out. Our lack of generosity becomes the proverbial cork in the bottle. The more you give, the more the door opens for additional resources to flow into your life. We are a missionary family. This year we gave away more than we earned 10 years ago. That's Jesus.

God has a hundred ways of getting resources to you. Maybe you signed up to go on a missions trip but you do not have the money. Do what you can, sell what you can, and let God fill up the remainder. Why? Because your giving has opened up the possibility of God's resourcing you.

One of things we love to do as a family at the end of the year is to ask Jesus how much we should give in the coming year. When you start doing that, it gets a bit scary. If a figure comes to mind that you can handle, you can be pretty sure it is from the devil. If it is a figure that you cannot absorb, well, when you begin to launch out it is amazing how God will pour resources into your life! This is for not only preachers or missionaries; this is for people who want to walk the faith life. This is for people who want to become a blessing to the community. This is for people who want to be an influence in the kingdom of God. God will meet your needs. The Scofield Bible says "all my needs." That includes everything that your needs might include.

Categories Not Included

There are, however, two categories the promise does not include. The first is the consequences of laziness. You know... the I'm-just-going-to-lie-in-bed-and-trust-the-Lord attitude. God will not bless laziness. In fact, 1 Thessalonians 3:10 says, *"God expects us to work. People who are unwilling (not unable) to work should not be given handouts."* That messes up our social system. The Bible says hard work produces a profit. We do what we do and God does what we cannot do. When we first started Next Level International, we only needed about £70 a day—and that was scary. Twenty years on we needed 40 times as much. We have found that the only way to make this work was to give more money away. That kind of faith primes the Source. There was a time that we had a financial crisis. One of our major supporters, who gave the ministry about $7,000 a month, rang up and told us that in three weeks no more money would be coming. Jesus must have money somewhere else then. I went to our bookkeeper and asked if there was any undesignated money in any of our accounts. She found $1,000. I said, "Great! We need to give that away immediately. I know a church planter in Egypt who needs a bit of cash. Can you wire it to him this week?" It is important to get seed in the ground immediately.

Over the next six or seven months, the whole thing turned around and the crisis was solved. When you get committed to this kind of life, you open yourself up to incredible blessing.

The Bible says God will meet our needs, but He will not meet our *greeds*. That is the second category. In 1891, a survey was taken in the United States, particularly among the pioneers who were moving west. About 5,000 settlers were asked to list their basic needs. The collected information indicated a list of 16 basic needs. At the end of the last century, a more extensive survey was carried out and the collated information indicated the number of basic things people said they needed to stay alive had grown from 16 to 92.

Generous on Every Occasion

Deuteronomy 8:18 says there are some people who are uniquely gifted to create wealth to establish God's covenant in the earth. Many of us are not gifted in that way. God does not want His children to have a survival mentality—an attitude where we just have enough to survive. The average Christian could not afford to be a Good Samaritan—putting someone up in a hotel for three days and paying the bill—because the credit card is jammed. The Bible says God wants you to be *"generous on every occasion."* [38] How can you be generous on every occasion if you have not made a way to be generous on every occasion?

I would like to change my attitude; to be a greater man of faith. Would you? God wants us to have *more than enough.* He wants us to have more than enough so we can be a blessing. Not to selfishly lavish it on ourselves, although the Bible says *"God... richly provides us with everything for our enjoyment."* [39] You do not need to feel bad if you have been blessed with a nice home and car. However, that is not the reason why we are alive. That is not the purpose for our existence. The reason we are alive is to advance the kingdom of God.

If you need to give yourself to study to advance the kingdom of God, get abundance in that area. If you are called to generate income for the kingdom, give yourself to that. Others have skills that they need to give themselves to. We have to go beyond where we are now. God wants to bless us so that we can become a blessing to others. In Genesis 12:1-3, God said to Abraham, *"I am going to bless you so that you can consume as much as you possibly can."* No, it doesn't say that. God did say, *"I am going to bless you... and all peoples on earth will be blessed through you."* This is having a life much bigger than our own.

This is where we find potential for pouring out our lives to touch other people. There will be people in heaven that you have never met because your generosity got them there. You did something so that somebody could hear about Jesus. The supply is according to His glorious riches in Christ Jesus.

There is No Pie

I find it interesting that some churches I visit have a pie mentality. They think there is a certain amount of money for missions, a certain amount for the general budget, a certain amount for social needs, and a certain amount for everything else. And when a piece of the pie is gone, there is only a fixed amount left. That is a non-kingdom mentality. *There is no pie!* The moment you give something away, you create an avenue for more to come into your life. *"The earth is the Lord's and the fullness thereof."* [40] When you understand this, you will discern that when you get a bonus at work it may be to help a ministry or to meet a need. It may not be for you at all.

The Bible says there are two kinds of seed that come to us: *seed to give and seed to eat.* [41] When you get that bonus, that tax rebate, that unexpected money coming in, you need to ask God if it is for you or are you to be a conduit of blessing. God is moving money around on the planet however He wants to because it doesn't belong to me. I enjoy everything, but nothing belongs to me.

One of the missionary families who used to work with us changed their car because they have a large family and needed a people mover. They thought they would trade that car against the newer one, but God said, "Give that car to the new missionary family that is coming in." That was Jesus making provision. If we could open ourselves to the possibility of being a conduit for God's blessing, we would find things would be radically different. We are not in a pie mentality; we are in an abundance mentality. There is no limit to God. We have the laws of nature screaming at us that there is more than enough to go around. Did you know that if wealth were distributed equally everybody on the planet would have $10 million U.S. each? There is more than enough. Eradicate the thought that you are diminishing your resource base by giving, and understand that you are increasing your resources by making space for more to come in. Just a thought.

Second Corinthians 9:8 says this, "Remember this, whoever sows sparingly will reap sparingly and whoever sows generously will reap generously. Each one should give whatever he has decided in his heart to give, not reluctantly, not under pressure, for God loves a cheerful giver." I cannot bend your arm to make you give anything. The only reason I want to inspire you to give is so that you can be blessed. I want you to understand the abundance of blessing that comes into our lives as you become generous.

The Macedonian and Corinthian churches gave again and again even though they were poor.

They learned what it was to be generous and as a result, they ended up with a life much bigger than the life they had. They helped Paul plant churches all over Europe.

Missions Giving

If you are not yet giving to missions, I want to encourage you to start. If you do not know where the funds are going to come from, let God solve that for you. Maybe some of you are already giving but you have gotten a bit static. It has become a budgetary item and there is no faith in it. The Bible says, *"Everything that does not come from faith is of sin."* [42] If it is just a budgetary item, you are actually sinning. We have to get into a place where Jesus has to come through for us. Look, I am just trying to make you into a *normal* Christian.

The Bible says, *"The righteous will live by faith."* [43] For those who do not have enough, or have just enough, God wants to help you. He wants to move you into *more than enough* so you can become a huge blessing in the kingdom of God.

Ever-Increasing Faith: Study Guide

Flight Plan

In this chapter we see a compelling argument for the necessity of a generous mindset and lifestyle if we expect to grow in faith. We discovered that God's promises are conditional; IF you, THEN He. We cannot lay claim to the promises of God if we are not holding up our end of the bargain. Below are a few quotes from this chapter. Take time to reconsider them and take note of the thoughts that bubble up:

"If we want to invoke God's blessing on our life, then we have to adopt a generous lifestyle."

"They actually saw their personal economic situations of lower importance than the needs of lost people coming to Christ."

"Sometimes resources are not flowing in because we are not letting enough flow out."

"If it [giving] is just a budgetary item, you are actually sinning. We have to get into a place where Jesus has to come through for us."

Take-Off

In this chapter there is a story of who men; John and Wayne, who end up at the pearly gates with Saint Peter together. John is led to a spacious mansion while Wayne is led to his heavenly "shed". Of course Wayne has issue with this and confronts Saint Peter on the obvious error. Saint Peter responded "we could only build with what you sent up, and you sent up so little." Can you remember the way you responded when you first read that story?

Giving when we don't have what we need doesn't make logical sense. The math doesn't add up. Three minus two is less, but in the Kingdom, three minus a gift is more! What needs to shift in our mindset and values for us to step into giving generously as a lifestyle? What hindrances or hesitations do you recognise in your own life?

Flight Crew

Discussion Questions:

1) What part of this chapter was most difficult to hear? Why?

2) What objections come up for you? Explore these honestly.

3) In what areas do you need to doubt the doubt?

4) What truths do you know from scripture that can help you step over these objections with confidence?

5) What do you need to start doing differently, immediately?

Captain's Log

Reflection: What questions do you have? What is hard for you to hear?

Journal Prompts: Journal honestly in a letter to Jesus about your thoughts and feelings. Then pause, bow in surrender, look at Jesus alone – What is He saying to you? Write it all down, don't stop to analyse, keep writing. Review and test what you wrote during your "Ground Control" time.

In-Flight Training

What is your next step in faith forward? Ask Holy Spirit now to give you a step of obedience to take in the area of giving.

1) What did He ask you to do? (Write down the specific directions.)

2) Who will you invite to this journey of faith with you as accountability and support?

3) When will you start giving?

Checking IN or Checking OUT?

Take a moment to listen to your inner dialogue as you consider the commitments you are making. What temptations to "check out" of these commitments do you see? What justification creeps in that allows you not to take this too seriously? What hurry, worry or fear knocks at the door? What power do you have available to you to deal with these enemy tactics? What will you choose when they confront you this week?

Will you check IN or check OUT?

Ground Control

Set some time aside for silence and solitude. Invite your Heavenly Father to speak to you by His Holy Spirit. Go back and read your captain's log from this week, your letter to Jesus and your honest thoughts and concerns.

What is the still small voice whispering to you now?

1) Write it down.
2) Test it. (Is it congruent with the nature of God and with scripture?)
3) Make it sacred; do not dismiss it, but take it seriously.

Soaring Higher

Take time with your journal and the Holy Spirit to navigate and confront potential strongholds in your life:

1) What conviction to you feel Holy Spirit pressing you on?
   a. Will you dare to ask Holy Spirit about this?
   b. What lie(s) are you believing that keeps you acting from objection vs faith? Can you repent honestly for believing this? Do so now.
   c. What is the Truth? Ask the Holy Spirit to reveal this

to you.

   d. What is your next step of obedience?

2) "If you don't have what you need, what you have is seed". What would your life look like to live like this? What is Holy Spirit saying to you about this?

3) There is no pie – Where do you see the "Pie" mentality showing up in your thinking? What is the root belief? What are you doing to do about it?

> *When you understand that God is your resource, incredible things begin to happen. You begin to see life through an abundance mentality.*

Maintaining Your Confidence in God

Fear knocked at the door and faith answered. No one was there.

- Old English Proverb

"Whatever happens, my dear brothers and sisters, rejoice in the Lord. I never get tired of telling you these things, and I do it to safeguard your faith. Watch out for those dogs, those people who do evil, those mutilators who say you must be circumcised to be saved. For we who worship by the Spirit of God are the ones who are truly circumcised. We rely on what Christ Jesus has done for us. We put no confidence in human effort...[44]"

When we consider the word *confidence* in this context, it does not mean being loud or brash. It does not refer to people who naturally have an effervescent personality or a positive, objective view on life.

Having confidence in the Lord means having a gut feeling that, when everything goes all wrong, you know it is going to be all right. When everything around you is collapsing—your dreams have not come to fruition and your prayers are not answered—you have an inner confidence, a gut feeling or an assurance that it is going to be all right. That is the kind of confidence that Paul writes about.

Let us contemplate some principles, which will help us maintain our confidence in the Lord. The Apostle Paul had many things he could put his confidence in; he points out several in verses 5-6. Yet, in the final analysis, Paul chooses to *"glory in what Christ Jesus has done for us."*[45] His confidence is not in his heritage, not in his experience, not in his religious pedigree, but ultimately and utterly in the Lord Jesus Christ. Yet how does one do that when things have not worked out?

Let us refer to a very familiar passage about David and Goliath in 1 Samuel 17. This chapter provides three insights that will help maintain our confidence in the Lord. The Israelites were engaged in war with the Philistines. David was sent to the Israelite camp by his father, with food for his brothers. After arriving at the army base camp, David witnessed Goliath coming out for his daily intimidation session—screaming, shouting, and carrying on.

King Saul is horrified, almost impotent, because he does not know what to do. Though David was only 17 or 18 years of age, he was stirred up because he realised the reputation of God was at stake. The character and nature of God was being tarnished by the taunts of Goliath.

Remember Past Victories

Verses 34-36 reveal keen insights into the character and confidence of David: "…but David persisted. 'When I am taking care of my father's sheep and a lion or a bear comes and grabs a lamb from the flock, I go after it with a club and take the lamb from its mouth. If it turns on me I catch it by its jaw and club it to death. I have done this to both lions and bears, and I'll do it to this heathen Philistine too, for he has defied the armies of the living God!'"

Notice that there is plurality in David's encounters. I used to read this passage thinking that there had been one lion and one bear. The language indicates that David had done this a number of times! Lions and bears, oh my! And he fought these battles in private. There was no army, no gallery, and no king to play to. He had been given a job to do and he did it with all of his might. Before we have significant public victories, we have to know what it is to have consistent private victories.

We live in a strange day where, unfortunately, the immature are trying to act like giant killers. We see people trying to take authority over demonic forces in cities and they do not even know when to turn off the television. They are endeavouring to pull down satanic strongholds and they do not know when to stop putting food in their mouths. If we want significant public victories, there have to be routine private victories. David had established a pattern in his private life.

We have to revisit the private, personal disciplines of the Christian life. I am on a crusade to make the Bible popular again, with Christians! People have time for DVDs, iPods, MP3s, and CDs but the Bible is still the supreme book. When I was 14, I had been saved for only 14 weeks when one of my school friends said to me, "How do you know the Bible? Have you read it all?" This so provoked me that I read the Bible all the way through. Since then, I have read the Bible through at least 70 times.

If you read four chapters a day, you can read the Bible in one year. Read 10 chapters a day and you can read the Bible every four months. Personal discipline helps us get back to the Book. If we are unable to do what we think menial and ordinary, we are already disqualified for the mighty and the spectacular.

We have to kill a few lions and a few bears. We have to learn to control the lust of the flesh, to overcome greed, fear, hurt, bitterness, and disappointment. These are the lions and the bears. These are the little skirmishes of life that we fight in private! These are not the honking huge battles; these are the preliminary prologues before stepping upon the main stage. Private victory comes before public victory.

One of the strong disciplines we established in our ministry is having small accountability groups. There was a time when someone asked me, "Ian, does your organisation have more influence than substance?" That was a difficult question because we can always do more things, plant more churches, train more leaders, take more teams; but substance is not increasing activity or getting busier. I decided that if we were going to have more substance as an organisation, then each individual must have more substance. The best way to ensure that we develop more substance was by putting ourselves in small accountability groups and committing ourselves to leadership life principles. We established accountability on two levels: on a work level and a ministry level.

Every two weeks we get together and spill the beans. We had to table our goals in four areas. We based it on Luke 2:52, where Jesus grew intellectually, relationally, spiritually, and physically.

Most of us were good at two or three areas, but most of us were not managing all four. As soon as you state your goals you are accountable for them. For example, "For a period in my life, my intellectual goal was to read two Christian books per month and to get better at the computer; my relationship goal was to date my wife every two weeks and my children once a month." These goals became accountability issues and the group held me responsible to follow through. When you travel as much as I do, the relational goals are a big challenge.

Our group decided not to verbalise the spiritual goals—pray more, read more, fast more—but to go for more conceptual goals. Such as, I want to know more about the righteousness of God or the holiness of God. The moment you start spelling out those goals, people send website links, articles, and emails. It is fantastic. My physical goal was to swim twice a week. It did not matter where I was in the world, the people in my accountability group were emailing me every week to ask how my goals were going. I could not escape! Unless we are growing personally, our capacity for ministry is diminishing daily.

When was the last time you did something for the first time? We complain that church is boring, the pastor is boring, and the ushers are boring. When was the last time you did something for the first time?

The first time you used a spiritual gift you were absolutely paranoid. You did not have time to be bored. You were calling on Jesus, praying for the Spirit's enabling and you were stretched well beyond boredom. New experiences have a way of keeping us fresh, vital and alive. If we want a high level of confidence in God, we have to supply fresh stimulus to our spiritual vitality.

In 1992, I was the National Youth Director of the Assembly of God churches in the UK. Our youth leadership felt led to bring Carman to the UK to do a tour. When I shared our vision with the executive council, they were nowhere near as excited as I was. They said, "Ian, how much is this going to cost?" I said, "Well, about $320,000 US dollars for five nights. I know that seems like a lot of money. But when we get the advertising out, we're going to be packed out." They responded to my word of faith, encouraging me by saying, "OK, Ian, you can do it, provided that you underwrite the first £40,000 of debt." That was not encouraging.

Against my wife's better wisdom, I decided to put our house up as collateral. We engaged in a massive advertising campaign and after one month, we had sold eight tickets. I realised that we might have a problem. We needed to sell 10,532 tickets to break even. I was feeling a little pressure.

When the week of the tour arrived, I was proactive. I started saying goodbye to our house. I began to tell Judith how fantastic it would be to live in a tent. For some reason, she did not agree.

That week, I did not need any encouragement to get up earlier than usual for prayer. I discovered that you only go to sleep during prayer times when you have nothing serious to pray about. I pored over the scriptures. I claimed promises. I told the Lord, "God, this was your idea. This was not my idea."

Toward the end of the tour, I got to the theatre in Manchester and the manager was swearing at me and going absolutely ballistic. "What is wrong with you people? For weeks, we had not sold any tickets, but the phone has been ringing off the hook and in the last 49 hours we have sold over 1,000 tickets." I felt like a champion. My house was no longer in jeopardy and we actually made a small profit for Jesus.

In 2007, our ministry needed £1000 a day to support 47 church planters and train 5,000 leaders across Eastern and Central Europe. Every year, our budget has increased and our faith has expanded. You might be thinking, "I would not like to live like that." That is why you are bored! I find it ever so difficult to be bored. When it is either Jesus or jail, it is difficult to be bored.

You might be thinking that I write a lot about money. I realise that we need faith for every area of life. Some of you have a passion for divine healing, so start with praying for a common cold or an achy elbow—start somewhere. Some of you have a passion for revival; pray for the salvation of your neighbour. If we have faith for the small things, God gives us faith, influence or power. We begin to build our spiritual muscle. If we want our confidence in God to grow, then we work from the small to the large, never the other way around.

David remembered his past victories. When you are in the arena and facing a giant obstacle, remind yourself how God came through again and again. Trust Him. Your history with Jesus is something in which you can place your confidence. Remember the past victories.

Remember Who You Represent

Goliath threatened David with his life. Verse 45 shows us how David responded to the intimidation of the enemy. David shouted in reply, "You come against me with sword and spear and javelin, but I come against you in the name of the LORD Almighty, the God of the armies of Israel, whom you have defied." David knew Whom he represented. He was God's man doing God's work. He was not representing King Saul or the Israelites. He was not a representative of the Bethlehem Chamber of Commerce, the Women's Auxiliary or the Jerusalem Slingshot Company. He told Goliath, "I come against you in the name of the Lord." [46] Do things your own way and you are on your own. Do things God's way and God will cover your back.

Several years ago, there was an economic collapse in Albania and the country was in chaos. People were raiding the army bases and eight-year-olds were walking around with guns. We had been planting churches in Albania and we had a missionary there. One day we got a call from the Foreign Office.

They knew we had a missionary in Southern Albania, and they asked if we wanted him out. "Yes," we answered, "but we cannot get him out." They said if we wanted him out, they would get him out. That was good. A day later, we received a call from someone high up in the SAS[47] asking if we wanted him out. We still wanted him out.

They knew the house he lived in and the bedroom he slept in. They asked if he would do what he was told. They told us to convey the following instructions. On Monday, he was to go 2 km north of the village to a bridge crossing a small stream.

At 8:00 a.m., two Land Rovers would come over the mountain, cross the bridge and turn around. He was to get into the second Land Rover that had a small Union Jack on the front bumper. It would look like a civilian vehicle, but it would be operated by armed military personnel. He was to get in and say nothing.

He was there at 8:10. The Land Rovers came over the mountain, turned around and picked him up. The vehicles took off, but were held up by a militia group. After hours of negotiation, one of the soldiers had a great idea. He decided to have a birthday party. Whose birthday was it? It was everyone's birthday.

They gave everyone presents: Scottish whisky and cigarettes. Later, another militia group stopped them and they did not want whisky, they wanted blood. After eight hours of negotiation, they finally got through. Twenty minutes later, they drove up into the mountains. Out of nowhere, three Chinook helicopters appeared. Two helicopters landed on the mountain, the backs opened up and 12 armed men came running out. They drove the Land Rovers onto the helicopters and took off. The missionary was airlifted to Italy.

Once he was safe, we get a call saying, "Your man is out safe and sound."

We all wondered, "Why is the British government using all these resources to get a little missionary like ours out of southern Albania?" Then, we realised that he was a British citizen with a British passport. There is only one thing better than a British passport and it is the passport of heaven. The Bible says our citizenship is in heaven, and when we do what Jesus tells us to, we have His resources covering our backs. When we know Whom we represent, we have confidence that God will meet every need.

Remember Who is on Your Side

David's statement to Goliath tells us something else. He was consciously aware that God was with him—God was on his side. He told Goliath, *"I come against you in the name of the Lord. Today the Lord will conquer you..."* It is the power of the Lord that will vanquish the enemy and slay the giant. But David had his part to play, as well. He said, *"... and I will kill you and cut off your head."* [48] He had to demonstrate his faith by taking Goliath's weapon out of his own hand and hacking off his head.

Several years ago, we had agreed to sponsor a conference in Romania. The conference had grown to 2,000 people and we agreed to host the conference and pay for the hotels and expenses.

Four months prior to the conference, the brothers rang me up to ask if we had the money to pay for the conference. I asked, "Do you need the money right now?" They said, "No, not yet." I said, "That is why I do not have any money." Two months later, they rang me again. They needed money for the deposit on the halls, so I sent it. With a few days to go, they rang me again to say, "We cannot get a tent to hold the main sessions in." I said, "You keep looking and I will keep praying." I was scheduled to preach in Calgary, Alberta for the weekend. After speaking, I went for lunch with the senior pastor. Across the restaurant, I saw a guy I had worked with for 12 years in the West Midlands, UK. He had done some ministry in Romania, so I went over to chat with him. I asked him if he knew anybody who had a 2,000-seat tent in Romania. He said, "Yeah, me." "Where is that tent?" I said. "In a city called Oradea," he replied. That just happened to be where our conference was! We can have confidence when are representing Jesus. He has a vested interest in getting the job done.

Friends, when our confidence has been shaken we can restore it by doing three things. First, remember past victories. Second, remember Whom we represent. Third, remember Who is on our side. If God is for us, the devil is in big trouble.

Maintaining Your Confidence in God: Study Guide

Flight Plan

In this chapter we grappled with the big vision of what God has called us to, the refreshing news of what we already have access to and the responsibility we must take to see it bear fruit in our lives.

"Before we have significant public victories, we have to know what it is to have consistent private victories."

"We have to revisit the private, personal disciplines of the Christian life."

In order for us to maintain our confidence in God we have to consistently remind ourselves of what is true, specifically:

1) Remember past victories

2) Remember who you represent

3) Remember who is on your side

Take-Off

This chapter confronted in plain terms our need to address the lust of the flesh, greed, fear, hurt, bitterness and disappointment in our lives. These are the lions and the bears before we face our Goliath. So often we want to rush past these difficult, glory-less, seemingly trivial issues in our lives to get to the good stuff, but faith is not built on rehearsed behaviours or rituals it is built on character. God wants to be able to trust our character in any situation He places us in. To become this, we must learn to trust his character and His ways. Ian said "Unless we are growing personally our capacity for ministry is diminishing daily."

Time to be honest. Rate yourself from 1 (Not at all) to 10 (It's a daily habit) on the following disciplines:

1) Prayer
2) Scripture reading
3) Exercise
4) Healthy eating
5) 7-8 hours of sleep
6) Time of intentional rest/Sabbath
7) Making your bed

8) Arriving promptly at meetings

9) Keeping your word

10) Turning off the TV/social media.

11) Giving generously

Is there one that jumped out at you or was loaded with Holy Spirit conviction?

Flight Crew

Discussion Questions:

1) Ian said: "If we are unable to do what we think is menial or ordinary then we are already disqualified from the mighty and the spectacular."

    a. What objections come to mind?

    b. What is your spirit yearning for?

    c. What causes us to follow our mind over our spirit?

2) David had to fight lions and bears before he could be trusted to face Goliath. Can you identify a lion or bear in your life presently? (lust of flesh, greed, fear, hurt, bitterness, disappointment etc.)

    a. How are you responding to it?

    b. Do you need to change your response?

3) Why do we have a tendency to overlook these things in our own lives?

    a. Why does this matter?

    b. What doors do we keep open for the enemy by refusing to address these issues?

Captain's Log

Reflection: What has your journey in personal self-discipline looked like? What areas have you seen victory? What contributed to that victory? What areas have your consistently hit a wall? What differences do you see in how you have tackled each one?

Journal Prompts: Take time to journal three times this week.

- **Day 1** What physical discipline do you struggle with most?
    - Have you asked Holy Spirit for insight into the matter? (lies or limiting beliefs you believe that keep you trapped.)
    - Have you asked other believers to help you?
    - What are you going to do about it?
- **Day 2** What mental/emotional discipline do you struggle with most?
    - Have you asked Holy Spirit for insight into the

matter? (lies or limiting beliefs you believe that keep you trapped.)

- ○ Have you asked other believers to help you?
- ○ What are you going to do about it?
- **Day 3** What spiritual discipline do you struggle with most?
    - ○ Have you asked Holy Spirit for insight into the matter? (lies or limiting beliefs you believe that keep you trapped.)
    - ○ Have you asked other believers to help you?
    - ○ What are you going to do about it?

In-Flight Training

Confront a "Menial" discipline. What is a habit or discipline in your physical life (eating, fitness, cleaning up) that God is asking you to address in your life?

1) Can you commit to 30 or 60 days of building a healthy habit in this area?
2) Who will hold you accountable?
3) How will you keep the mindset of experimenting vs success/failure in this?
4) When will you start?
5) How will you invite the Holy Spirit to help you?

Checking IN or Checking OUT?

Take a moment to listen to your inner dialogue as you consider the commitments you are making. What temptations to "check out" of these commitments do you see? What justification creeps in that allows you not to take this too seriously? What hurry, worry or fear knocks at the door? What power do you have available to you to deal with these enemy tactics? What will you choose when they confront you this week?

Will you check IN or check OUT?

Ground Control

Set some time aside for silence and solitude. Invite your heavenly Father to speak to you by His Holy Spirit. What thoughts bubble up? What is the still small voice whispering to you?

1) Write it down.

2) Test it. (Is it congruent with the nature of God and with scripture?)

3) Make it sacred; do not dismiss it, but take it seriously.

Soaring Higher

Dig into the gospels. Where can you find evidence that Jesus had some habits and rituals in "menial" things that governed His life?

> *We can have confidence when we are representing Jesus. He has a vested interest in getting the job done.*

Seizing Your Destiny

No act of kindness no matter how small is ever wasted.

- Aesop (c.620-560 BC)

Paul, an apostle of Christ Jesus by the will of God, to the saints in Ephesus, the faithful in Christ Jesus: Grace and peace to you from God our Father and the Lord Jesus Christ. Praise be to the God and Father of our Lord Jesus Christ, who has blessed us in the heavenly realms with every spiritual blessing in Christ.[49]

Would anybody like to learn to live generously? You have got to *be* generous to *be generous*. The Apostle Paul knew how to be generous whether he had a lot or whether he had a little, or as The Message puts it, "hands full or hands empty." In this chapter, I will share stories that describe generosity from both perspectives.

I have the opportunity of preaching in numerous countries, different conferences and churches, and at times it is quite challenging because everyone has a different take on things. I preach in places where they argue over whether God wants to bless them; they debate about it. "Am I good enough, holy enough, Baptist enough, charismatic enough, evangelical enough, Catholic enough?" This incredible debate goes on. I have to tell you, we have been blessed with every spiritual blessing in Jesus Christ. Friends, understand something about your eternal destiny: you will have faith to walk in God's favour, because you are *already* a blessed person. Moreover, if God never did another thing for you, you are already incredibly blessed. Your sins have been forgiven, your destiny is secure, and the blood of the cross works for you every day of your life. God has given you the Holy Spirit to testify with your spirit that you are born again. You have a spirit inside you that would cry, "Abba Father." You are a blessed person.

The Bible says, *"Greater is He that is in you than he that is in the world"* and you know what that means—it makes us believers a scary bunch of people. We are blessed. Unless you begin to believe that you are blessed you will always be wondering, "Am I good enough, strong enough, wise enough, and good looking enough?

Do I have the right shades, the right clothes, the right

aftershave? Did I shower?" When you understand that you are blessed, you have faith, faith to walk in God's favour. What we accomplish for God is not because we are clever or because we have a technical edge. We do what we do because we are an incredibly blessed group of people.

When we have a sense of eternal destiny, Reinhard Bonnke says, "We are condemned to victory." We have to work hard at losing because we have so much going for us! You are blessed. First Samuel 2:30 states, *"Those who honour Me, I will honour."* That word "honour" here literally means *weight or weighty*. It means, "Those who put their weight behind Me, I will put My weight behind them." How would you like the weight of God behind you? I need the weight of God behind me financially. If we honour the Lord with the tithes and offerings, will He not open the windows of heaven upon us and pour out a blessing that we cannot contain?

Some of you are tithing but you are not getting the second part of that scripture, the blessing, because you are doing it like a slot machine. You are putting your money on the plate as it comes past on Sunday morning, but you are not mixing faith with it. It is almost as insignificant as putting Monopoly money in the offering.

The Bible says, *"The just will live by faith."* And we give by faith, recognising it is a supernatural exercise, not just going through the motions of putting some paper notes in the offering plate.

Some time ago, I was in church after having missed two months because I had been away. I put two lots of tithes in the offering and that really hurt. But I had major needs so I was calling on heaven, saying, "God, I am calling resources to meet my need."

The Bible says, *"Whatsoever a man sows, that will he reap."* The Bible talks about sowing and reaping in 2 Corinthians 8 and 9. These chapters talk about money. You cannot spiritualise these chapters because they will make absolutely no sense. It is talking about money using an old agricultural illustration. The farmer sows and then he reaps. When we give our tithes and offerings we sow and we reap. What a man sows that will he reap.

Imagine a farmer who has had a terrible harvest, what will he do in the spring? Is he going to get just a handful of wheat and carefully put it into the ground? That would be hopeless! No, he's going to grab all the wheat he can possibly get and ram it into the ground because he knows he needs a honking big harvest.

Because of the way I live, my family sometimes has no money. I need to clarify that—no money means NO money. For some people, that means they left all of their cash at their house and have nothing with them right at this moment. I mean no money. There have been times I am about to jump on a plane when there are a wad of bills to pay. Judith will say to me, "What are we going to do about these?" *The unwritten rule in our house is, when we have no money it must be time to give.* I had to ask myself, "What do you sow when you have no money?" One time I went to the wardrobe, pulled out a suit, got on the plane and went to Romania. I found a little Romanian pastor and said to him, "I need to give you this suit in Jesus' name." He responded, "Ian, that suit is too big for me." "Well," I replied, "Perhaps you and your brother could wear it."

I have given away watches, shirts, shoes, and all kinds of other things. I have to put seed into the ground to produce the harvest. Unless we begin to get the spirit of this, you will find yourself confessing what you don't have. You are confessing lack, lack, lack. If you want some more, give something away.

I want the weight of God behind me financially. We have to break this spirit of lack, of poverty, and of poor- mindedness. We can change the generation of young people that are rising up in the name of Jesus. We can change them to be a normal, generously outrageous, giving group of people. If you want the weight of God behind you, you are going to have to give beyond your tithes and offerings.

Some people do not understand that actually God wants to put His weight behind their job. God put an anointing on Joseph to succeed in a secular climate. There are business people who have a vision to start companies and businesses and that desire has come from the Lord. God is saying to you, "I want to put My weight behind you." When you understand your blessing, you have faith to walk in God's favour. It is not faith in how good you are, or how well you perform. No, it is His favour; it is the outrageous favour of God. I have what I have by the grace of God. It has come to me and I am highly blessed. And I refuse to be embarrassed. We always said to our missionary staff—and at that time they all were living by faith like myself—you are going to be better off working here than you ever were working in any church because Jesus always pays better wages than churches. It's just a thought. When you have a sense of eternal destiny, it will get you to be fruitful in your God-given gifting.

My most favourite verse in the whole Bible is Ephesians 2:10: *"We are God's own handiwork, His workmanship, created in*

Christ Jesus so we might do good works which God has predestined, pre-planned before and for us." When we understand what we are created for, then we actually have faith to believe we are going to succeed. God doesn't make failures; God creates people who are able, capable, anointed, gifted, and able to succeed in the area that God has placed them. You are that person. You are that person—not the person behind you, not the person on the other side of the town. You are that person. When you understand that there is destiny all over your life, then you expect to succeed in what God has called you to do. It is not my plan and it is not your plan. It is His plan and He actually has a vested interest in it working. He gave the blood of His Son that it might work.

Many years ago, God gave us a vision for our missions organisation at that time, Next Level International (NLI). In my heart, I knew that we were going to plant hundreds of churches. I knew that. We were going to train 10,000 leaders; we were just going to do that. We were going to see thousands of people released into short-term missions. It was going to happen. God has committed to it happening. Why? Because when I do what I am doing, I know I have God's favour on my life and I can expect to be fruitful in my God-given gifting.

Some years ago, I was in Melbourne, Australia. I met an Australian business man, a gentleman by the name of Dan Daniels. When he was 23 years of age, he went to a conference in Adelaide. On the last night of the conference, the essence of the speaker's message was: It's time to make money for Jesus because we've been making money for ourselves for far too long. At the end of the service he asked, "Is there anybody here that wants to make money for Jesus?" Dan Daniels stood up. The preacher came down from the platform and said to him, "Young man, you are going to make millions and millions and millions of dollars for Jesus. You are going to send the gospel to the four corners of the earth." Well, Dan was so excited he was absolutely flick- flacking on the inside. He could hardly wait to get home and see his wife. He told his wife what the preacher said but his wife was nowhere near as excited. She responded, "Love, that's great, but you borrowed money for the plane ticket just to get to the conference and we have got bills to pay. So please return from Planet X."

He had one idea in his mind: how to destroy medical waste that is produced in hospitals. He presented his idea to a number of companies in the northern areas of Australia that were already involved in that business but they all thought his idea was absolutely stupid.

He couldn't get anybody to buy it. So he went back home and made a prototype machine in his garage. It took him two years. When he had a first dry run, he realised that his machine was 30 percent more efficient than the machines currently on the market. He decided to bid on contracts on that basis. He won one or two contracts, and started to have a bit of cash flow. Then he got the machine made properly and it was about 40 percent more efficient. Within seven years, he had gained 85 percent of the Australian medical waste market. Well, that was a bit of luck wasn't it? I would like to suggest to you that he happens to be moving in his God-given gifting. Dan said to me, "Ian, you are passionate about winning lost people. You want to get people saved, and you want to establish churches.

I am passionate about making loads and loads and loads of money for Jesus." There are people that need this message: they were born to become resource agents to move the kingdom of God mightily forward. When we move in our gifting and our anointing, things come to us, we make connections, and things begin to happen. Why? We have faith and confidence because we know our destiny. What about it? Will you live in your gifts and your anointing?

Your Highest Priority

When you have a sense of eternal destiny, it will demand your highest priority. I frequently have the opportunity to meet with people in Eastern Europe. According to our standard of living, they have absolutely nothing, and yet they are so incredibly passionate. They are consumed with their destiny. Sometimes, however, I return home on the plane thinking, "My God in heaven, am I saved? I have just been with people who walk two hours every Sunday just to go to church. They *walk* two hours to go to church. I have just been with people who go without food for three or four days for the kingdom of God to advance."

I remember arriving at one of our training conferences in Romania. We had faith to sponsor 1,200 people—hotels, train fares, food, and conference expenses. We told the people running the conference, "When you reach 1,200 people, that is it. If you have faith for more than 1,200 you can pay; we will only pay for 1,200." When I got to the conference and was checking into the hotel, I noticed a group of people in the corner mulling around. They started to move towards me. They said, "We want to see the green man." Being the incredible hulk that I am, I said, "Yes, I am Ian Green." They said, "We got a letter from Vasyli that told us we could not come to the conference, but we have come.

We have come from southern Romania where it is absolutely bankrupt and barren of all spiritual life. Ian, you know how to train leaders and how to plant churches; we do not know that. We are hungry for God to do something. Ian, we do not need a bed for this conference. We're happy to sleep outside – there are some benches, there are trees out there. We may get a little cool, but we have coats we can wear. We do not need any food – the conference is only for four days. You might be interested to know that some of us went without food to buy our train tickets. Let us tell you about Eduardo. His family felt he should come but he had no money for the train ticket. So the family decided—the whole family including six children, family members from ages five to 90—that if they went without food for a whole week there would be enough money to buy the train ticket." At this point, I was freaking out on the inside, but they didn't let up. "Ian, we do not need a bed and we do not need food, but what we do need is the Word of God. Ian, whatever you decide, don't deny us the Word of God." Flippin' heck. What was I going to say? "Clear off"? There were 60 people.

When you are exposed to that level of passion, it does something to you. Of course, we told them they could attend. We did not know where we would find beds or the money but we simply could not turn them away.

I remember sitting in a youth pastor's house in the centre of Budapest, Hungary. I had known these fantastic people for years. They were involved in an inner-city ministry so the church had very little money. They lived at the back of the church in a spare room. When they wanted to go to the toilet, they would go down by the front of the church and up to the right. When they wanted to cook a meal, they would walk down and take a left into the church kitchen. They lived like that for six years. I was in their room, and the room was small. They had pullout beds that were set in during the day, but at night, they pulled them out. They had an eight-month-old baby and a little cot for him to sleep in. The room was completed by a small round table with three seats. We were talking over dinner and I said to them, "Guys, you have got to get out of this room. This is flipping ridiculous. I am sure God honours you for living like this, but for the sake of your child this is inappropriate. You have got to get out."

They said, "Ian, we want to move out, but our salary is so small it just can't happen at the moment. Anyway, you don't know our story do you?"

"What's your story?"

"We dated for four years before we got married. We both had jobs in the days where you could buy a two-bedroom apartment for about $4,000 US. We do not want you to think we were extravagant in wanting a two-bedroom flat, but we have the gift of hospitality and we wanted people like you to come and stay with us. We were about ten days from our wedding and had saved enough for the apartment that we wanted. Then one night we both had a dream, independent of each other. As our custom was, we would meet two or three times a week in the city for coffee. That was the day after our dream. We met together and were both sombre and silent. By sheer intuition, we knew we had both had the same dream. I said to her, 'Did you have the same dream?' 'Yes,' she said. 'What do you think it means?' 'I think the Lord wants the money for the apartment.' Very practically she said, 'Did you ask Him how much He wanted?' 'Well,' I said, "I think He wants it all.'" And then they gave me some context about their area.

Up to that time, the Christians in Hungary had not had the opportunity to do evangelism for over 40 years. But that summer, 10 contracts had been given to go to cities where there were no churches. A truck and a sound system, lighting, and chairs had been provided. All that was needed was $4,000 US for literature and Bibles, and to advertise the event.

It was very hard for this young couple; it was as if their dream of a home had evaporated. They reminded themselves that they had given all they owned to the Lord.

They went to see the Pentecostal pastor and put a little bag on the desk. "Here's the money." The pastor asked, "How much is in the bag?" "About $4,000 US," they replied. The pastor started shaking and said, "I have been up all night praying. We have everything we need for the outreach, but we still needed $4000 for literature and Bibles and now you come up with it."

I was incredibly moved by this story. Every time I tell their story, I feel like the sword of the Lord is going through me. What would you do? How far would you go? How much would you give? She said to me, "Ian, ask us, would we do it again?" I looked around the room and asked. She replied, "Absolutely, of course, we'd do it again. We'd do it again, and again and again because right now in 20 cities in Hungary, there are people who are born again and attending church, new churches have been started because we gave up our two- bedroom apartment."

When you sense destiny inside of you, then you make it your highest priority and jettison every small dream you have got.

Seizing Your Destiny: Study Guide

Flight Plan

We have heard the cliché "what would you do if you know you couldn't fail?" We as Christians often forget that we are working from a place of pre-paid victory! The battle is already won, our inheritance as children of God is already secured, our access is guaranteed and the power and resource we need is in exhaustible. We are already blessed. This is a significant shift from a poverty/lack mindset to an abundance mindset and this shift is critical for faith to germinate and grow in our lives. Some quotes from this chapter to reconsider:

"Friends, understand something about your eternal destiny: You will have faith to walk in God's favour, because you are already a blessed person."

"Some of you are tithing but not getting the second part of

the scripture, the blessing, because you are doing it like a slot machine. You are putting your money on the plate as it comes past on Sunday morning, but you are not mixing faith with it."

"When you sense destiny inside of you, then you will make it your highest priority and jettison every small dream you have got."

Take-Off

In this chapter we read the story of Daniel, a man who wanted to make money for the Kingdom. He had one idea: how to destroy medical waste that is produced in hospitals. From there it took time, it took effort, it took money to take that idea and turn it into a money generating idea.

Just like faith starts as a seed and grows. The calling and destiny God has for us, comes to us in a form of a seed. One idea, that when we apply our small mustard seed of faith to it, it grows. The seed grows our faith, the faith grows our seed and the cycle continues until God's Kingdom comes, our character is transformed and everyone exclaims "How good is your God!"

"When we move in our gifting and anointing, things come to us, we make connections, and things begin to happen. Why?" Faith. Faith that God has a destiny for us. Faith in who God is and his ability to see us through.

If we need to put the seed in the ground to see a harvest, then what is stopping you from taking that step, and the next step?

Flight Crew

Discussion Questions:

1) "You are already blessed" is this easy or difficult to embrace? Why or why not?

2) What responsibility comes with the understanding "you are already blessed".

3) If we are to reap what we sow, we should get good at sowing – in what areas do you see yourself withholding vs sowing? What story is your life really telling when you withhold? Is that the story you want to tell?

4) How do you undermine a mindset of lack/poverty in your life?

5) God never hands us our destiny – he instead gives us a seed – and idea, an anointing and expects us to sow it, water it and nurture it to harvest. What seed of destiny has

remained neglected in your life because you felt you didn't have what you needed?

6) What do you need to do differently to walk in faith?

Captain's Log

Reflection: "Am I good enough, strong enough, wise enough, and good looking enough?" We often find comfort in inadequacy, but living a faith-filled live means confronting this apathy and driving out the insecurities.

Journal Prompts: Take time to journal with Holy Spirit and explore areas you feel inadequate or not good enough.

1) Where have you accepted inadequacy as reality?

2) What truth does Holy Spirit want to give you to counteract these lies?

3) What responsibility do you need to embrace to walk forward?

In-Flight Training

Ask Holy Spirit for a step of obedience in watering the anointing he has already placed in your life. What should you practice every day to water that seed?

1) Journal about it this an allow Holy Spirit to define the action you need take.

2) Who will you invite to hold you accountable?

3) When will you start?

Checking IN or Checking OUT?

Take a moment to listen to your inner dialogue as you consider the commitments you are making. What temptations to "check out" of these commitments do you see? What justification creeps in that allows you not to take this too seriously? What hurry, worry or fear knocks at the door? What power do you have available to you to deal with these enemy tactics? What will you choose when they confront you this week?

Will you check IN or check OUT?

Ground Control

Set some time aside for silence and solitude. Invite your heavenly Father to speak to you by His Holy Spirit. What thoughts bubble up? What is the still small voice whispering to you?

1) Write it down.

2) Test it. (Is it congruent with the nature of God and with scripture?)

3) Make it sacred; do not dismiss it, but take it seriously.

Soaring Higher

What is God calling you to? What book or resource do you need to dig into to help you become an expert in that area? What will you do to continue to learn in your area of anointing?

> *The Bible says "Greater is He that is in you than he that is in the world" and you know what that means – it makes us believers a very scary bunch of people. We are blessed.*

Living Generously

That's what I consider true generosity: You give your all and yet you always feel as if it costs you nothing.[50]

- Simone De Beauvoir, French Social Theorist

In his farewell address to the Ephesian elders, Paul quotes a well-known phrase credited to the Lord Jesus, *"It is more blessed to give than to receive."* The Good News Translation says it this way: *"Remember the words of the Lord Jesus Himself, 'There is more happiness in giving than in receiving.'"*

The Bible has hundreds of different themes. In fact, if you did a word search, you would find the word *believe* is mentioned 275 times in the Bible. The word *prayer* is there 371 times. The words *love, loves,* or *lover* are used 714 times.

However, you will find the words *give* or *giving* are used 2,162 times, and I have counted! My question may seem obvious: Where does the Bible put its emphasis? It is clearly on giving. Giving is an integral part of our Christian life. The Bible says, *"Give, and it will be given to you. For with the measure you use, it will be measured to you."* [51] The question is, what do we receive when we give? What is the *measure* that is returned to us? I want to answer that question by outlining the seven benefits of living the generous life.

Giving Makes Me More like God

You see, God is a giver. One of the first Bible verses most of us learned was John 3:16: *"For God so loved the world that He gave..."* The Bible says that when we become Christians, we become partakers of the divine nature. [52] God's nature comes into us when we are *"rescued... from the kingdom of darkness and transferred...into the Kingdom of his dear Son."* [53]

Because God is a giver, the desire to give begins to percolate inside of us more than ever before. God's generous nature begins to reshape our innate selfishness and greed.

As we give, we are expressing the Jesus that is inside of us. So, whether we give our time or our talents or our money, we are manifesting Jesus in our daily lives. Giving makes us more like God.

Giving Draws Me Closer to God

In the Old Testament, the concept of *giving of your substance* refers to giving from the heart.[54] The first five chapters of Leviticus—worth reading particularly if you cannot sleep—describe the five principal offerings that people brought to the Lord: the burnt offering, the meal offering, the peace offering, the sin offering and the trespass offering. Every time the people brought an offering, they had to make a special journey to the tabernacle. Their offering was like a magnet drawing them to the presence of God. When we begin to give of our substance, we are not buying our way into the presence of God. We are being drawn into the presence of God because we are giving some of the substance of our life back to Him.

Jesus said, *"Where your treasure is, there your heart will be also."*[55] For many of us, the most valuable commodity in our lives is money.

Money buys the things we need and like—the clothes that we wear, the homes that we live in, the holidays we enjoy and the food we eat. But what do we treasure? Is our heart attached to our substance, our things, our money? Or is our heart attached primarily to God?

Jesus said, *"You cannot serve both God and money."* [56] If we are reluctant to give things away, we may be more attached to them than we think. We may be living for things rather than the Lord. Jesus said, *"Freely you have received, freely give."* [57] Giving draws us closer to God because God is a giver.

Giving Gives Us Victory Over Materialism

There is a huge lie in our modern culture that tells us that you can purchase happiness. If you follow that thought to its logical conclusion, the person who has the most things should be the happiest. Hollywood is a mile square of greater Los Angeles County, and it is where the rich, famous and infamous live. Yet, there are more suicides per capita in that one square mile than anywhere else on the planet. You might think, "That is ridiculous! They have everything. They go to the trendy parties, are seen with the people that matter and live like royalty.

They can go anywhere, do anything and see everything." Materialism does not equal happiness. It is often a thin veneer which covers despair and loneliness. Every time we give, we break that spirit of materialism. Why? *"It is better to give than to receive."*

When we learn to give, it gives us victory over materialism. The Bible says, "Command those who are rich in this present world not to be arrogant nor to put their hope in wealth, which is so uncertain, but to put their *hope in God, who richly provides us with everything for our enjoyment."* [58] When the Bible says "those who are rich", that means all of us. There are few of us that will not have dinner today. When we get up in the morning, we will switch on the fireplace, make coffee, and have breakfast. Compared to many people in the world, even those of us with moderate incomes are rich. Should this statement make us feel guilty because God has blessed us? No, what we have received is a result of God's grace and mercy. The purpose of this statement is to engender thoughtful generosity. The passage goes on to say, *"Command them to do good, to be rich in good deeds, and to be generous and willing to share."* Open-handed generosity destroys arrogance and greed.

John V. Taylor, in his book *Enough Is Enough,* suggests that Christian families should go on a campaign. When the adverts come on the telly, or even when commercials are shown on TV, we should train the family to all jump and say, "You have got to be kidding!"

I like that. We have to beat materialism into shape. Rather than getting sucked into a selfish attitude promoted through a relentless media assault, perhaps we can aspire to a Higher-Selfless-God-first Biblical standard? Deuteronomy 14 teaches that the purpose of tithing is to always put God first in our lives.[59] Giving the first tenth of our income back to God is a reminder that He is our source.

Giving Strengthens My Faith

At one time or other, we have all felt that we cannot afford to give. We have heard the offering announced and had the following thought go through our minds. "Not this week, Lord, I can't afford it. You understand that, don't You Lord? I'm in a flippin' major mess; I can't do it." Giving when we cannot afford it strengthens our faith. The Book of Malachi says, *"Bring all the tithes into the storehouse... I will pour out a blessing so great you won't have enough room to take it in! Try it! Put me to the test!"* [60]

Now I have to be honest with you. Sometimes I am a little surprised how long it takes to see the blessing poured out! I wish it were like a vending machine—you put money in and you get coffee out. Thirty years of serving Jesus have taught me that it does not work this way. God is not indebted to me. *"Those that trust the Lord,"* the Bible says, *"will not be put to shame."* [61] Yet, with every promise, there is a premise. We say, "Lord, You give to me and I'll give to You." No. No. No. The premise is that we give first, as an act of faith, and then God will respond.

Martin and Ros Steel, from New Zealand, were missionaries for a number of years with us in Europe. Their family has a policy about summer camps. Martin and Ros would pay for the first camp, but beyond that, the children paid the camp fees. Their daughter Amy wanted to go to a second camp, so she decided to have a car boot sale. She was going to sell the soft toys and dolls that she did not play with anymore to raise the money, selling them out of the trunk of the family car. Around the same time, we were collecting items for people in Serbia, particularly children with significant needs. On hearing about this, Martin said to Amy, "You know, Amy, the children in Serbia would really appreciate those toys.

Why don't you pray about it and see if Jesus wants you send those toys off to Serbia?" She said she would. Amy decided to give her toys and we took them with us to Serbia. We gave them to Pastor Saleem for distribution. One of the other pastors asked where the toys had come from and Martin shared the story. He had also said to Amy that if Jesus wanted to meet her need in another way it would be a great faith builder. That pastor responded, "That is fantastic! How much is that camp?" The fee was $50, but the pastor gave Martin $100—which covered the fee and spending money. That was lucky, wasn't it? No, that was Jesus! It is wonderful when the turnaround is quick like that, but sometimes it takes time.

The Bible says, "Trust in the Lord with all of your heart, do not depend on your own understanding; honour the Lord with your wealth and with the best part of everything you produce. Then he will fill your barns with grain, and your vats will overflow with good wine."[62] The premise: "Trust in the Lord." The promise: "He will fill your barns." Sometimes, however, it takes an entire growing season to see the overflow. If it took more than one growing season, would you still trust God? Just a thought.

Giving is an Investment in Eternity

When we give to the furtherance of the gospel, or to meet needs within the community, we are investing in something with eternal value. When the money leaves our hands, it is working, it is functioning and it is active and alive. Our blessing, our love and our prayers are attached to it. We are making an eternal investment. Jesus said, *"Don't store up treasures here on earth, where moths eat them and rust destroys them, and where thieves break in* and steal. Store your treasures in heaven, where moths and rust cannot destroy, and thieves do not break in and steal. Wherever your treasure is, there the desires of your heart will also be."[63]

Giving Makes Memories

The Bible says, "A generous man will himself be blessed, for he shares his food with the poor."[64] The psalmist said, "Good will come to him who is generous and lends freely, who conducts his affairs with justice. Surely he will never be shaken; a righteous man will be remembered forever."[65] What are people remembered for? Calvin Coolidge, President of the United States (1923-1929) said, "No man is ever honoured for what he received in life; he is only honoured for what he gave."

When I think of Mother Teresa, my first thought is of a woman who gave away her life for the poor. I do not think of a woman who received the Nobel Peace Prize. I think of a model human being who selflessly gave to aid and help the poorest of the poor for decades. We are remembered only for what we give.

Giving Blesses Me

One of the motivational gifts listed in Romans 12 is the gift of giving. People with this gift organise their life and their means so they are able to give, give, give. I met an Australian millionaire who had the gift of giving. At that time, to conserve on his expenditures, he drove a 1983 Toyota. His colleagues would say, "You can't go to meetings in that car. You are going to buy that company for millions of dollars but they won't believe you have any money. You should also rent a suit for the day so they think you're credible!" People who have the gift of giving are often frugal in certain areas so they can be generous in others.

Most of us, however, have other gifts. Yet, we can still learn to be generous. Someone once said, if you are going to err, err on the side of generosity. There is great blessing when we give.

"Good will come to him who is generous and lends freely, who conducts his affairs with justice. Surely he will never be shaken; a righteous man will be remembered forever." [66]

"A generous man will prosper, he who refreshes others will himself be refreshed." [67]

Have you learned the principle of reciprocation? Whatever you give out you are going to get back. If you dispense criticism, you will be criticised. Give out anger and anger will come back at you. Be kind and you will receive kindness. Be loving and you will receive love in return. Be generous and you will receive generously. The refreshing that God brings, however, often comes from a completely different source. Some people always seem to land on their feet, regardless of what happens to them; when hard times come, they still seem to be alright. When we see people continually doing well like this, we need to understand what is under their feet and what they are standing on. An attitude of giving will probably be operating in their lives.

Giving Makes Me Happy

Jesus said, *"You're far happier giving than getting."* [68] In the Christian life, we occasionally give until it hurts. Occasionally. But we do not want too many of those experiences. It is far better to laugh when you are giving. The New Testament church was hilarious in its giving; believers were ecstatic, they jumped on the chairs, they shouted, waved their cheques and said, "Man, it is time for the offering.

Yahoo!"

I find I receive great pleasure in giving time, money and resources. I like to do it because I am doing what Jesus is expecting me to do. He is expecting me to be a giver. And when you do what He tells you to do, you are bound to be blessed. The feel-good factor is obliged to follow.

There are two types of people in life: there are the takers and there are the givers. Which one are you? When you turn up at church on Sunday morning, remember that someone else bought your seat, paid for the electricity and supplied the heat. Most of us were not there when the church building was built. But at some future point, we will have the opportunity to sow into the next project, mission or ministry.

Someone has sown into us so we can receive ministry and blessing. We must move beyond the taking stage and become givers. Are you smiling? Jesus said that giving makes us happy. Why? When we open up our hand to give, we are participating in the divine nature, the life of God is flowing through us and that will make us happy.

Jesus put it like this, *"If you try to hang on to your life, you will lose it. But if you give up your life for my sake, you will save it."*[69] Life does not begin at 20, 30, 40, or 50; life begins when we give our lives away. Different people on different parts of the road of life will receive different insight regarding what this means. Keep progressing along the road of generosity. Keep on going.

Do not back off. Do not keep stopping to count the cost. We have counted the cost and we are moving on. We are a group of people who are going to live generously for the kingdom of God.

Living Generously: Study Guide

Flight Plan

In this chapter we read about all the benefits of living generously. This chapter described the life we all want, but the means to obtaining it for some reason we are oddly resistant to. God desires to prosper us, he wants us to have the best, most adventurous, most meaningful, most fulfilling life possible. This often does not look at all like the comfortable, effortless life of bliss and ease we all take a prosperous life to mean. It's time to look under the hood of what a truly meaningful life is made of. Consider these quotes from the book again:

"As we give, we are expressing the Jesus that is inside of us."

"Open-handed generosity destroys arrogance and greed."
"if you are going to err, err on the side of generosity"

Take-Off

'If someone pulled you aside with a sales pitch promising something that would provide all these benefits:

1) makes me more like God

2) draws me closer to God

3) gives me victory over materialism

4) strengthens my faith

5) is an investment in eternity

6) makes memories

7) blesses me

8) makes me happy

- Would you buy it?
- How much would you pay for it?
- Does this sound too good to be true? Why or Why not?
- What is this magic thing? Giving.

Let's be honest, for most of us it does sound too good to be true, but God is good and gives good gifts so why should it be too good? God wants to hold nothing good from us. The issue comes when we value lesser, perhaps more immediate and more material things over the eternal good that God has for us. In doing this we short circuit our inheritance and rob ourselves of the very things that are both meaningful and eternal.

Flight Crew

Discussion Questions:

1) What was your first reaction to reading/discovering that giving accomplished this whole list of "benefits" in our lives?

2) If this is true, why do we hesitate to participate in generous living?

3) What aspect of our culture has influenced our mindset around generous living?

4) What do we need to do about it?

Captain's Log

Reflection: From the list of "benefits" of giving, which one was hardest to believe? Why? What other ones caused you to tighten your hand? Why?

Journal Prompts: Take time to answer the following questions in your journal for each "benefit" that was hard to swallow.

1) What have a believed about giving that was false?

2) What strategy is the enemy seeking to employ in my life with these lies or false beliefs?

3) What is Holy Spirit saying to me about this right now?

In-Flight Training

What do you need to do differently moving forward in the area of giving (Be specific)? Ask Holy Spirit now to give you a step of obedience to take.

1) What did He ask you to do? (Write down the specific directions.)

2) When will you start experimenting?

3) Who will you invite to this journey of faith with you as accountability and support?

4) When will you start?

Checking IN or Checking OUT?

Take a moment to listen to your inner dialogue as you consider the commitments you are making. What temptations to "check out" of these commitments do you see? What justification creeps in that allows you not to take this too seriously?

What hurry, worry or fear knocks at the door? What power do you have available to you to deal with these enemy tactics? What will you choose when they confront you this week?

Will you check IN or check OUT?

Ground Control

Set some time aside for silence and solitude. Invite your heavenly Father to speak to you by His Holy Spirit. What thoughts bubble up? What is the still small voice whispering to you?

1) Write it down.
2) Test it. (Is it congruent with the nature of God and with scripture?)
3) Make it sacred; do not dismiss it, but take it seriously.

Soaring Higher

"Every time we give we break the spirit of materialism" What is the larger principle behind this statement? How does this apply in your life? What can you give away today to help you break the spirit of materialism further in your life? "Sometimes, however, it takes an entire growing season to see the overflow. If it took more than one growing season, would you still trust God?"

Reflect and journal about where you see the desire for instant gratification or immediate results sabotaging faith and trust in your life. What decision do you need to make as a result of this reflection?

There are two types of people in life: there are the takers and there are the givers. Which one are you?

Waiting for a Miracle

"I realised that the deepest spiritual lessons are not learned by His letting us have our way in the end, but by His making us wait, bearing with us in love and patience until we are able to honestly to pray what He taught His disciples to pray: Thy will be done."[70]

— Elisabeth Elliot, Missionary

Life throws curve balls at us. Life is not a level playing field. Life is challenging. Because of the difficulties life throws at us, we may reduce our expectations without even noticing. We tone things down to the level of our own competencies, our own skill sets, our own experience, our own paradigm, and we end up with a life that is relatively small.

I want to raise your expectations. Jesus has a much bigger

life for you. When we think about life, what are we expecting? When we think about our family, our spouse, our children and our vocation, what are our expectations for them? What is the mental picture that comes to mind when their name is mentioned? What kind of enthusiasm explodes inside when we hear the names of the most loved people in our life?

If our expectation has not been realised, we feel disappointed. This is normal and is something we have undoubtedly experienced many times. Our lives are filled with stories of God's interventions. But we have just as many stories of God not turning up when we thought He should have. What I have learned over the past 30 years in my walk with Jesus is this: when things get bad, they normally get worse before they get better. Can you identify with that? There were times when you thought you were at the bottom and things only got worse.

Think of the children of Israel. They were slaves in Egypt for 400 years. That was bad. Then God raised up Moses to lead them out of slavery to the Promised Land. That sounded good. However, the people moaned and complained, so things got worse. Their 11-day journey to the Promised Land ending up taking 40 years.

197 | P a g e

Think of Jesus on Good Friday: he was arrested, mocked, flogged and crucified. That was bad. The Messiah was dead and the dreams of the disciples had vanished. Saturday was even worse. The officials sealed the tomb and placed armed guards to keep people away. The disciples feared for their own lives and went into hiding.

The honesty of the Bible is refreshing. The saints of God experienced the same disappointments that we do. They experienced the darkest hours of discouragement just before the dawn of hope. We need to learn from their example how to respond to disappointed expectations and discouraging circumstances. Few people experienced more setbacks than the Apostle Paul.[71] Yet he learned how to respond to bullying and persecution. He wrote to the church at Philippi, from jail, *"Don't fret or worry; instead of worrying, pray."*[72] That is the choice that we have to make. Either we worry or we pray. *"Let petitions and praises shape your worries into prayers, letting God know your concerns. Before you know it, a sense of God's wholeness, everything coming together for good, will come and settle you down. It's wonderful what happens when Christ displaces worry at the centre of your life."*[73]

Stop Worrying

We have to decide what to do with worry. Some people worry out of habit. Some worry when there is nothing to worry about. "It's been at least three hours and nothing bad has happened. Something must be wrong. Gosh, something bad is sure to happen soon." We can create a personal culture of worrying. Worry can become part of our DNA. There is an alternative, however. We can make prayer and faith a part of our DNA. We decide: are we going to worry or are we going to pray and have faith? When we turn worrying thoughts into prayers, we invite the grace, the presence and the power of Jesus into our lives. Here are some prescriptive scripture verses to help you overcome worry:

"Cast all your anxiety on Him because He cares for you."[74]

"Give all your worries and cares to God for He cares about what happens to you."[75]

Jesus said, "That is why I tell you not to worry about everyday life."

"Give your burdens to the LORD, and he will take care of you. He will not permit the godly to slip and fall."[76]

In Luke 8, the leader of a local synagogue had a daughter

who was ill. He went to Jesus and said, "I've really got a problem, Jesus. My daughter is very ill; in fact she is dying." Jairus poured out his heart and obviously believed that Jesus could heal his daughter. Yet, Jesus got distracted. While Jairus was describing his daughter's infirmity, someone had touched Jesus and power had gone out from Him. There was a lot of commotion, which likely took a considerable amount of time. This was undoubtedly frustrating to Jairus who had a palpable sense of urgency.

That happens in our lives too. We are praying and believing but nothing is happening. At the same time, people around us are being blessed. They are being healed, getting promotions at work, taking fantastic holidays and buying new cars.

Then for Jairus, it went from bad to worse. While Jesus was preoccupied with the woman who had been healed from a hemorrhage, "A messenger arrived from the home of Jairus, the leader of the synagogue. He told him, "Your daughter is dead. There's no use troubling the Teacher now."[77] For Jairus, it got worse on a number of different levels.

First, the answer did not come quick enough. Second, the person with the answer appeared to forget about him. Third, others were being helped while his daughter died. You can imagine the discouragement Jairus felt. He had done the right thing. He had come to the right person. It seemed to be the wrong time.

Things like that happen on this journey of faith. Jesus said on another occasion, *"In this life you will have tribulation."* [78] He said offences would come. Difficulties and challenges are a part of living on the planet. Years ago, people used to say, "When you come to Jesus all your problems will disappear." My gosh, the advertising council would nail us against the wall for that. No, no, no! I personally found that my troubles increased when I became a Christian. The difference was I had someone to walk with me through the troubles. I have Jesus walking with me, standing with me, helping me, whispering to me and encouraging me. When life looks black and dark, inside me there is a still, small voice that says, "It is going to be all right, just trust Me."

In the midst of the commotion, Jesus was told that Jairus' daughter had died. Jesus made His way through the crush of people to find Jairus. Jesus said, *"Don't be afraid. Just have faith, and she will be healed."* [79] That was pivotal.

What Jesus was saying was, "What are you going to vote for Jairus? Will you vote for the problem or will you vote for My promise?" Jairus waited patiently for Jesus and saw a breakthrough – the miracle of his daughter coming back to life. When you are waiting for a miracle, the first thing is not to worry. The second thing is to change your focus.

Change Your Focus from the Problem to the Promise

In 2 Chronicles 20, Jehoshaphat and the men of Judah were being assaulted by the combined military forces of the Moabite army, the Ammonite army had hired mercenaries. The enemy was vastly superior. Intelligence came to Jehoshaphat that they were advancing and preparing to attack. This struck fear into the heart of King Jehoshaphat. He called for a nationwide fast and set himself to seek the Lord. He prayed: *"But now, here are the men from Ammon, Moab, and Mt. Seir, whose territory You would not allow Israel to invade when they came from Egypt. So, they turned away from them and did not destroy them. See how they are repaying us by coming to drive us out of the possession You gave us as an inheritance. O our God, will You not judge them for we have no power to face this vast army that is attacking us. We do not know what to do but our eyes are upon You."* [80]

Jehoshaphat did not know what to do militarily, but in another sense, he did. He turned his eyes to God.

When you need a miracle, there is nothing better that you can do. Turn your eyes upon Jesus. Turn to His Word. Let your eyes focus on the promises of God. Let the truth of God's Word change your point of view. Place worry under the authority of the promises of God. *"All the men of Judah, with their wives and children and little ones, stood before the Lord. Then the Spirit of the LORD came upon Jahaziel son of Zechariah, the son of Benaiah, the son of Jeiel, the son of Mattaniah, a Levite and descendant of Asaph, as he stood in the assembly. He said: "Listen, King Jehoshaphat and all who live in Judah and Jerusalem! This is what the LORD says to you: 'Do not be afraid or discouraged because of this vast army. For the battle is not yours, but God's."* [81]

Why did the writer of the Chronicles provide a lengthy lineage for this man? Jahaziel was a man from a well-known family with a noble pedigree. Asaph had been a close associate of King David and he was the author of numerous psalms. [82]

When the word of the Lord came in prophetic form, it came from someone who had proven himself reliable and trustworthy. They could trust the encouragement: *"Do not be afraid or discouraged because of this vast army. For the battle is not yours, but God's."*

They began to move their eyes from the vast enemy that was about to obliterate them to the promise, *"I will never leave you nor forsake you."*[83] Their hearts, which had been filled with fear and dread, now swelled with confidence. They trusted in the word of the Lord and it completely changed their attitude and their point of view. It hardly needs saying that they were victorious: God did it all.[84]

Fear Not

It has been said that there are 365 *fear nots* in the Bible; one for every day of the year. Jeff Kusner has written a book entitled "Fearful to Fearless" and published a helpful website 365FearNots.com.

Actually, there are slightly over 100 such verses, but the book and website contain over 400 scriptures pointing us towards a fearless Biblical lifestyle. There are in excess of 3,000 promises in the Bible. The promises have to be claimed. When God gives a promise, it is like a cheque written in our name. We can keep the cheque on a shelf collecting dust or we can lock it up in a desk drawer. We obviously receive no value from the cheque until it is signed and deposited. One of the ways in which we sign the cheque is by praying the promise back to God. Prayer is not persuading God to do something that He does not want to do. God has already made up His mind about the miracle that you need. Have you made up your mind? Sometimes we can hold back what God wants to do because we have not made up our mind. The Bible says, *"A double-minded man is unstable in all of his ways."* [85] Here is how we can pray the promises of God. There are times when we are called on to enter an environment where we feel insecure—maybe a new job, new role or new position. Whenever we are out of our comfort zone, we can turn to 2 Timothy 1:7 which says, *"For God has not given us a spirit of fear and timidity, but of power, love, and self-discipline."* [86]

We can pray, "God, I thank You that I do not have a spirit of fear. I thank You that I have a spirit of love, power and a sound mind. I thank You for that." I apply the promise to my situation and pray it until the promise takes root in my spirit.

We have the promise of companionship. Joshua 1:5 says, *"I will never leave you nor forsake you."* Jesus repeated this promise to the disciples in the New Testament.[87] We can feel isolated or separated. "Jesus, thank You that You never leave me. Thank You that as I sit at my desk, You are sitting with me. As I pick up my tools, You are with me." I pray back the promise to God.

We have the promise of help. Psalm 46:1 says, *"God is our refuge and strength, an ever-present help in trouble."* God is going to help in our time of deepest need.

We have the promise of provision. The great instance of God's provision is Genesis 22:8, where God himself provided the sacrifice—saving Isaac's life. How many of us have discovered that after a miracle offering, in which we give the largest single gift of our lives, our finances can get worse? We thought they should have gotten better, but they got worse: our investments slide, the car breaks down, the washer blows up and your spouse burns the salad.

We take the promise: "Jesus, I don't understand what is happening but I understand You are the One who provides. I am not going to dictate how You are going to provide, I just know You are going to provide. If I need wisdom to make my money stretch further, if I need a promotion, God I know that You are the provider."

As the Holy Spirit confirms the promise to our spirit, we will have more difficulty disbelieving than we do believing. The truth has taken root inside of us and we have a growing trust in God's provision.

Although circumstances have not changed, people have not changed, the bank balance has not changed, yet we know it will be all right.

Give Thanks

The third thing we have to do when waiting for a miracle is give thanks. First, stop worrying. Second, change our focus from the problem to the promise. Third, start giving thanks for what we do not yet see. Hebrews 11:1 says, *"Faith is the confidence that what we hope for will actually happen; it gives us assurance about things we cannot see."* You see, praise is the language of faith. It is the articulation of what God has done and will do in your life.

Let us go back to 2 Chronicles. Through Jahaziel the Lord said, "Tomorrow march out against them and you will find them coming up through the Ascent of Ziz, at the end of the valley that opens into the wilderness of Jeruel." This sounds bad but it gets better.

"But you will not even need to fight. Take your positions; then stand still and watch the LORD's victory. He is with you, O people of Judah and Jerusalem. Do not be afraid or discouraged. Go out against them tomorrow, for the LORD is with you!" Then King Jehoshaphat bowed low with his face to the ground. And all the people of Judah and Jerusalem did the same, worshiping the LORD."[88]

Their confidence was at such a high level that what was happening in the physical world was irrelevant. They knew in their hearts that the victory God was promising the next day had already transpired in the eternal world. It was going to be all right because the Lord was with them. It was the Lord's battle.

When we start to give thanks, it gets God working in our circumstances. On one occasion, I felt crushed by a number of different things that were happening in my environment. I created a four-hour space and slapped some praise and worship on. I began to verbalise praise and adoration to Jesus.

I began to exalt the name of the Lord. The issues had not changed, but as I began to break through in praise and worship and articulate the promises of God's Word, I felt life, faith and vitality. Nothing had changed, but I had changed.

As we praise, we start releasing the will of God to work in our environment. We become convinced of His will. We are not *persuading* God we are *cooperating* with God. We are not praising God *for* the circumstances; we are praising God *in* the circumstances. The result is that the peace of God comes to our heart. When we make a decision not to worry, when we refocus from the problem to the promise and we start praising, the peace of God rises up like a guard around our hearts. When unbelief tries to sneak in, the peace of God is surrounding your inner person.

These very simple thoughts can transform your inner world and will ultimately transform the world you live in. If you are waiting for a miracle or an intervention, if you are waiting for God to turn up, I want you to tell the Lord. Stop and tell Him how. It may be a financial miracle, a relational miracle, some difficulty at work or some challenge you are facing. Begin now by saying, "God, I need You. I am not going to worry. I am going to apply the promises of Your Word to my situation. I am going to praise You in advance for what you are going to do."

Father, I thank You because You are the God of miracles. You are the God of restoration, care and love. Father, I now trust You in the name of Jesus that You will do what You have promised You would do. Amen.

Waiting for a Miracle: Study Guide

Flight Plan

We all have experienced seasons of waiting, deferred hope and unfulfilled expectations. If we linger in that disappointment however, we will find that our faith lowers to meet our expectations instead of rises to meet the character of God. In this chapter we are challenged to confront the disappointed expectations and complex circumstances with faith using four simple, but not always easy Kingdom strategies.

1) Stop worrying
2) Change your focus from the problem to the promise
3) Fear not
4) Give thanks

Is living from a place of faith really possible even when things around us seem to point in another direction?

What does it mean to put our faith in the character and nature of God vs an outcome? How do we find hope amid the very real emotions and pain? Be encouraged to open your heart to hope and healing as we get ready for take-off. Consider these quotes from the chapter again:

"We decide: are we going to worry or are we going to pray and have faith?"

"God has already made up His mind about the miracle you need. Have you made up your mind? Sometimes we can hold back what God wants to do because we have not made up our mind."

Take-Off

In this chapter we find a fresh look at the story of Jairus, a leader of the local synagogue whose daughter was very ill and on deaths door. Take time to read the story afresh from scripture in Luke 8:40-56. A desperate father has a lead on hope, the man who has been healing so many is in the neighbourhood. He begs for the healer's attention and his heart leaps when Jesus turns to follow him. But the crowds want Jesus attention, they are all clamouring for Him to attend to their urgent need as they crowd around him. Suddenly the healer stops. He gets distracted, He starts looking for someone.

Grief must have leapt into Jairus heart. "Please hurry the time is short, you are my only hope. I know if you come now you can save my daughter." While the healer is distracted, Jairus' servant arrives to tell him it is too late. She's gone. Hopes dashed. THAT woman robbed him. WHY did Jesus get distracted? IF ONLY...

We see and recognise the emotional rollercoaster Jairus must have gone through, but how many times have we read this story and missed what he must have gone through. Reading it in shallow terms, glossing over the pain and disappointment that surely was present in this moment. This is a moment most of us have lived out in one situation or another. The outcome was not what we expected, yet the end for Jairus was not the end for Jesus.

What was impossible for Jairus, was not a limitation for Jesus.

How often do we give up hope in light of circumstance instead of put our hope in the God who deals in the impossible? What needs to change in how we approach difficulty and disappointment?

Flight Crew

Discussion Questions:

1) Why is a clear understanding of the nature and character of Christ critical for our faith?

2) In what ways can circumstance and disappointment cast a shadow over how we see God?

3) How do we guard our heart and guard the truth about who God is when confronted with worry and fear?

4) Of the four steps presented in this chapter, which is most difficult for you, and why?

5) Stop Worrying

6) Change your focus from the problem to the promise

7) Fear not

8) Give Thanks

What strategy will you use to change?

Captain's Log

Reflection: If worry, problem centric focus, fear, and lack of gratitude are fruits of an earthly heart/mind, what are their kingdom counterparts? Take time to reflect on your life. Where do you see yourself functioning from the flesh vs from the Spirit?

Journal Prompts: Take four days this week to journal and respond to what God is stirring up in you:

Journal: Day 1 What step of courage is Holy Spirit inviting you to take?

Journal: Day 2 What makes you hesitate to obey?

Journal: Day 3 What do you stand to lose?

Journal: Day 4 What will you do about it?

In-Flight Training

Identify which of the following you struggle most with:

1) Worry/anxiety

2) Problem centric focus

3) Fear

4) Lack of gratitude.

Ask Holy Spirit for a step of obedience to practice to starve out the earthly mindset and nurture your confidence in who God is.

1) Who will you allow to hold you accountable?

2) When will you do it/Start?

3) When will you know the Kingdom mindset has taken over?

Checking IN or Checking OUT?

Take a moment to listen to your inner dialogue as you consider the commitments you are making. What temptations to "check out" of these commitments do you see? What justification creeps in that allows you not to take this too seriously? What hurry, worry or fear knocks at the door? What power do you have available to you to deal with these enemy tactics? What will you choose when they confront you this week?

Will you check IN or check OUT?

Ground Control

Set some time aside for silence and solitude. Invite your heavenly Father to speak to you by His Holy Spirit. What thoughts bubble up? What is the still small voice whispering to you?

1) Write it down.
2) Test it. (Is it congruent with the nature of God and with scripture?)
3) Make it sacred; do not dismiss it, but take it seriously.

Soaring Higher

Read 2 Chronicles 20, the story of Jehoshaphat. In your journal note where do you see discouragement, disappointment, defeat or anger in your response to God regarding your circumstances.

1) Has an expectation that God will take away the challenges crept into your theology?

2) How has that impacted your ability to respond to God in faith and trust?

3) What do you need to repent of? Pray a prayer of repentance now.

4) Can you make the decision "I don't know what to do, but my eyes are on you God?" If so, invite the Holy Spirit to give you fresh insight on how to walk in this way. What truth do you need to hold on to?

As we praise, we start releasing the will of God to work in our environment. We become convinced of his will. We are not persuading God; we are cooperating with God.

The *"Whats"* of Life

Christians can have doubts and they can have questions, and the
unhealthy way to deal with that is to keep them inside where
they fester and grow and can undermine our faith. The healthy
way to deal with it is to talk about it and be honest
about it.[89]

Lee Strobel

"In a little while you will see me no more, and then after a little
while you will see me." Some of his disciples said to one another,
"What does he mean by saying, 'In a little while you will see me
no more, and then after a little while you will see me,' and
'Because I am going to the Father'?" They kept asking, "What does
he mean by 'a little while'? We don't understand what he is saying"
(John 16:16-18 NIV).

The context of John 16:18 takes place during the closing week of Jesus' life. The disciples were confused about the future: "What does this mean? *A little while* – we don't understand what You are saying." Have you noticed? Jesus is brilliant at giving people just enough information so that they do not understand. Like the disciples, we might find that frustrating because we have yet to understand the greater plan of God in our lives.

A *what* of life had hit the disciples. Their expectations of what was going to happen were rapidly evaporating. They thought Jesus was the Messiah and that He had come to set up His kingdom. He was going to rule from Jerusalem. He was going to bring to an end the Roman domination of the land and a Messianic reign would follow. As the disciples got nearer to the cross, they did not understand how the cross fit into the plan. And because they didn't understand, a *what* hit their lives and left them utterly confused.

"What was that?"

I remember the first time that someone close to me died tragically. No reason, no rationale. A 22-year-old Bible College student, married with two children, was putting his tools in the boot of the car when another car came from behind and crushed him against his own vehicle. I still do not know how to answer that *what* because it seems such an incredible waste of a life. A person with so much opportunity, so much potential and a *what* hits.

Like many, I was grieved by the devastating tsunami that hit Asia on December 26, 2004. What really rocked me was that only three days afterwards, they were putting deck chairs back on the beach in Thailand. That was shocking to me. Hours before, dead bodies were floating everywhere. But it seemed that all the people were concerned about was getting their life back to normal.

What is normal?

I was recently involved in a course where we were challenged to think about how pictures hang on a wall. When you go into a room and see a picture hanging askew, you want to go and straighten it so that it is hanging symmetrically to the wall. We were asked, "Who told us that pictures have to hang straight?" Life teaches us that. In the same way, when life goes askew, we want to put it straight again. That, however, is not always possible. As much as some of us do not like change and do not like our world being askew, it is not going back to the way it was. Yet, in the redemptive purposes of God, He can bring incredible good out of chaos. Am I saying that I believe Jesus killed my friend? No. But I do believe that some redemptive purpose will come out of that tragedy.

We have to look at the redemptive purposes of God during the challenging seasons that we find ourselves in. God is with us; we are not bereft, we are not orphans. The statement of Jesus, *"I will never leave you nor forsake you"* [90] is still true. When the *what* hits us, we have to be open, not to the answer, but to the purpose that God is trying to bring to our lives. I want to talk about several *whats* we encounter in life. But it is important to understand that Jesus doesn't always give us the answer we want.

The silences of God are often articulating His purposes in a more profound way than would the answers to our questions.

Forgiveness

The first *what* is the *what* of forgiveness. What do we do when someone damages us in some way? We have a choice: forgiveness or unforgiveness. Forgiveness opens the door to the redemptive purposes of God in our life. But let us understand clearly the characteristics of forgiveness.

1) It includes full and free acquittal from the offence.

2) It assumes no obligation from the offender to the offended.

3) Forgiveness is an act of the will, not an act of the emotion. Most times, we do not feel like forgiving the offender. We want to withhold our forgiveness as a way of punishing the other person. We have no right to do that. The Bible says that if we do not forgive, then we

   a. will not be forgiven.[91] That means that we are the only

   b. ones who suffer if we fail to forgive.

4) Forgiveness includes praying blessing on the person who has offended you.[92] No one said this is easy, but Jesus did not leave us an option. "God I pray for incredible blessing upon that person's life. I pray for richness, I pray for Your goodness, Your mercy, Your kindness, and that all their steps will be blessed of the Lord. I pray that they will discover You in a greater, more wonderful way." When you begin to pray like that, you slam the door on unforgiveness creeping in the

   a. back door of our lives.

5) Forgiveness includes expecting God's best for that person.

a. When we apply these insights, we begin to eliminate unforgiveness.

The Repentance KGB

What forgiveness does not allow us to do is evaluate whether or not our offender has genuinely repented. Forgiveness is not dependent on the offender's repentance. We all want to see the *fruit of repentance*[93] in the offender's life. But we are not the Repentance KGB shining a bright light into the person's face, trying to find out if they are telling the truth or not. Ultimately, Jesus is the only One that can judge the person's heart—we have no right or permission to do that. When we have been offended and have not forgiven the offender, if we see the person or even think of them we can be tempted to relive the offence over again in our own minds. We replay the conversation; we remember the weight of words and the punctuation that actually punctured our lives. That would be a reasonable indication that we have not fundamentally dealt with the offence.

Forgiveness, or dealing with the offence, does not include the restoration to the former level of relationship and trust. We have forgiven, but it is not back to business as normal. There may be months and years of re-establishing and rebuilding trust. We have still forgiven them, it is just that we have to build and repair levels of trust.

There may be instances where it's not feasible or possible to rebuild levels of trust, for safety reasons, or because of geographical limitations or for other reasons. If that's the case, that's OK. Sometimes forgiveness can mean the end of a chapter; in some cases, a relationship may not be re-buildable. But we still have to forgive. These are some of the things we must consider when we walk the walk of forgiveness.

Anger

The second *what* that may hit us is the *what* of anger. I don't know about you, but in this season of life, I have found myself often incredibly angry. Up until this point, I am normally only very angry in airports. Judith tells me, "You would not have to fly so much if you would only learn to control your anger in airports. You are not *smelling the coffee*; you are not *waking up*. Don't you understand the redemptive purpose of God in airports is not for you to get from A to B, it is actually to learn to control your anger." These wives, I don't understand them.

Some of the realities about anger are that anger is a secondary emotion. That means that anger frequently piggybacks on other emotions; it does not usually stand alone. Oftentimes anger will piggyback on hurt, or frustration or fear. Therefore, when anger is erupting in our lives, we have to ask ourselves, "Why am I angry? What is going on here? Am I fearful of something, am I frustrated about something, am I hurt about something?"

Anger is often attached to those other emotions and, of course, we all have capacity for anger. We sometimes talk about people having a short fuse. Do you know what? Anger is permissible.

In fact, if you read about Cain and Abel in the Old Testament you will discover that Cain killed Abel because he was angry, very angry. God did not rebuke him initially because of his anger, Genesis 4:7 tells us, he was rebuked because he did not *control* his anger and how it was expressed. The New Testament also tells us that there is a kind of righteous anger that is not sin.[94] But righteous anger is not our problem, it is the other kind.

Boiling over in rage is not OK or permissible. I am not saying it has not happened, I am not saying I have not experienced that—I have experienced that. The expressions of anger *can* come under control. We have the ability to change; we are not helpless. We have the power of the Holy Spirit to dominate the flesh part of anger, the unrighteous anger that we have often excused.

What I am saying is there is a redemptive action in the power of the cross that can enable us to create choices of where we are going to channel our anger. Proverbs 14:16 puts it like this: *"A wise man fears and departs from evil, but a fool rages and is self-confident."* When anger boils up, ask the Holy Spirit for help.

Fear

The last *what*, the *what* of fear, smacks us right between the eyes. Job 3:5 says, *"What I've always feared has happened to me. What I've dreaded has come to me."* Incredible fear. There are all kinds of fears that have erupted in my heart. I have struggled with the fear of failure. I have had to say to Judith, "Is this a good marriage?" I have had to talk with incredible honesty.

Many of you who are married have questioned the level of your own marriage. We have had to ask, because you can drift through life and presume everything is okay. There is the fear of not having, the fear of death, the fear of what others think, the fear of abandonment – there are many possible fears. This is what I have learned to do with fear:

First of all, I categorise it. Sometimes fear comes in a general way and you cannot deal with it unless you identify it.

Secondly, you have to face it. I face it with scripture and I start to intimidate that thought. I say something like this: "I am not giving into that. I am not bowing down to that fear. I am not giving in to that emotion. Jesus says, 'I will build My church and the gates of hell will not prevail against it."[95]

Summing it up

When the *"whats"* of life hit us, we have to look deeper and understand the redemptive purpose of God. First, we are beginning to discover what is important. I have done some pretend gold mining in South Africa.

They give you a little sifter and then you have to get all the junk, rubbish and sand out. Then all the little nuggets of gold supposedly come to the top—well, they look like gold, but they are fake! Jesus is trying to help us to understand what is ultimately important by sifting things in our lives. Remaining constant and firm to the vision that God has called us to is fundamentally important.

Second, we must grow beyond where we are. When the *"whats"* of life hit us, we have to understand that God's redemptive purpose is for us to become bigger people on the inside. We are not just fitting into the crowd; we are actually growing on the inside to move towards full maturity in Jesus Christ. *"Consider it a sheer gift, friends, when tests and challenges come at you from all sides. You know that under pressure, your faith life is forced into the open and shows its true colours. So, don't try to get out of anything prematurely. Let it do its work so that you may become mature, well developed and not deficient in any way."* [96]

Father we thank you for the truth of your Word. We pray, Lord, for these scanty bits of information to take root in our lives. We pray that as we consider all kinds of "whats" that hit us that we may be able to stand and become fully developed in your redemptive purposes in Jesus' name. Father, we ask You again for Your kingdom to come, and for Your will to be done and for Jesus to be highly exalted and for lost people to pour into Your kingdom. We are asking for an increased breakthrough anointing upon our community that we may be brokers of hope, that people may have a chance, that people may have light at the end of their dark world to engage with You. In Jesus' name, let Your kingdom come and Your will be done. Amen.

The *"Whats"* of Life: Study Guide

Flight Plan

Accidents, disease, natural disasters, pandemics, economic collapse, war; the list of "whats's" are a mile long. Sudden issues that challenge what we thought was supposed to happen. None of us are exempt from these events in our lives, but how we respond to them impacts our lives and faith greatly. In fact, how we respond to these situation tells us if we actually understand who we are in Christ and who God is in our lives, or not.

So often when disaster or painful circumstances strike, our first response is to look to God for rescue. In this chapter however, we are challenged not to look for rescue, but for purpose. God is not the author of awful, but he never wastes it when it inevitably shows up in our lives. God's purpose and desire to form us into the image of Christ and have the power and glory of Christ revealed in and through us in every situation is the bigger vision for our lives.

This higher purpose is not easy, but it is powerful, and when we open our vision and our hearts to the higher purpose of God our faith ignites, our hope is restored, and the impossible becomes possible in our life. Consider these thoughts from this chapter again:

"But I do believe that some redemptive purpose will come out of that tragedy"

"The statement of Jesus, 'I will never leave you or forsake you' is still true."

"We have the ability to change; we are not helpless. We have the power of the Holy Spirit to dominate the flesh part of anger, the unrighteous part of anger we have often excused."

Take-Off

In putting our perspective on the more important things of the Kingdom; our maturity and living out our calling we allow God to sift out from our lives that which is lesser and unimportant and retain what is of greatest and eternal value. Our character is eternal, our activity is temporal. The condition of our hearts and mind expressed in faith is way more significant than our rituals and religious behaviour. Take time to read the scripture from James 1.

Do we look at our painful trials through the lens of opportunity and joy? Do we allow the painful circumstance to accomplish the job of maturation and purification in our lives? Can you think of a scenario you are going through right now that God may want to use for these greater purposes in your life?

Flight Crew

Discussion Questions:

1) In what areas of our lives does fear, anger, or unforgiveness have a stranglehold on us?

2) Can you identify the higher purpose God is calling you to in this situation?

3) How does understanding our identity in Christ help us with this?

4) Why is it hard to confront anger, unforgiveness and fear in our lives?

5) What do we stand to lose if we do not deal with these things in our lives?

6) Can you share a story of overcoming in one of these areas?

Captain's Log

Reflection: Reflect on the excuses you have made in the past, or perhaps are making now in regards to dealing with anger, fear and unforgiveness. In what ways do these excuses influence your decision making? What are you losing as a result?

Journal Prompt: Take four opportunities this week to review and debrief your day. Each day, ask yourselves these questions, journal your responses.

1) Where did I see fear, anger or unforgiveness show up in my day today?

2) How did I respond in the moment?

3) What undealt-with things lies under the surface that I need to confront?

4) What do I need to repent for? What do I need to let go?

5) Who will I choose to become? What characteristic of Christ will I choose to embrace today?

In-Flight Training

What is your next step in faith forward? Ask Holy Spirit now to give you a step of obedience to take.

1) What did He ask you to do? (Write down the specific directions.)
2) When will you start experimenting?
3) Who will you invite to this journey of faith with you as accountability and support?
4) When will you start?

Checking IN or Checking OUT?

Take a moment to listen to your inner dialogue as you consider the commitments you are making. What temptations to "check out" of these commitments do you see? What justification creeps in that allows you not to take this too seriously? What hurry, worry or fear knocks at the door? What power do you have available to you to deal with these enemy tactics? What will you choose when they confront you this week?

Will you check IN or check OUT?

Ground Control

Set some time aside for silence and solitude. Invite your heavenly Father to speak to you by His Holy Spirit. What thoughts bubble up? What is the still small voice whispering to you?

1) Write it down.

2) Test it. (Is it congruent with the nature of God and with scripture?)

3) Make it sacred; do not dismiss it, but take it seriously.

Soaring Higher

Reflect on the statement of Jesus that says "I will never leave you or forsake you". Journal your responses to the following:

1) When was a time that you did not believe this?

2) What expectation did you put on the Father in this moment?

3) What lie did you come to believe as a result of the expectation or disappointment?

4) Often we put our faith in an outcome vs in the nature and character of God. Was this applicable in this circumstance?

5) In hindsight, what purposes did God achieve through

that circumstance?

6) What have you learned?

> *We have to understand that God's redemptive purpose is for us to become bigger people on the inside.*

Faith to Walk in Darkness

Now, God be praised, that to believing souls gives light in darkness, comfort in despair.

- William Shakespeare, Henry VI, Part II

"Who among you fears the Lord and obeys the word of his servant? If you are walking in the darkness, without a ray of light, trust in the name of the Lord and rely on your God. But watch out, you who live in your own light and warm yourselves by your own fire, this reward you shall receive from me: you will lie down in great torment."[97]

I want to talk about what happens when God turns the light out. It is important to understand that this passage is talking about a believer in God. It is someone who has faith; they have come alive to God and they are walking in the ways of God.

The text says they fear the Lord, they obey His Word and

yet they find themselves walking in darkness. I want to talk about why we find ourselves in spiritual darkness and how to respond. First, however, let me briefly list three additional causes of darkness of which we need to be aware.

Sin

Darkness comes into the life of a believer for many different reasons. There is a darkness that comes because of sin. The Bible says, *"Men loved darkness instead of light because their deeds are evil."* [98] Let me tell you, if you are struggling in the dark with some private, personal, secret sin, it is difficult to get victory over that. The moment you drag it into the light, you discover that the sin loses its power because it cannot stand the light. Some people say to themselves, "I am going to get over it, I am not going to tell anybody, I am going to struggle through." My friend, it does not work like that.

There is a darkness that is produced as a result of sin. People make crazy decisions when they are shrouded in the darkness of sin. Whether it is rebellion, self-centredness or conceitedness, when we live in an atmosphere of sin, our mind becomes deranged and we make ridiculous decisions. That is a form of darkness.

Ignorance

There is a darkness because of ignorance. In Ephesians 5:8, the Bible says, *"For once you were full of darkness, but now you have light from the Lord. So live as people of light!"* That means that God wants us to walk in wisdom not in the darkness of ignorance. When we do not understand God's way, when we do not understand God's plans, when we do not understand God's Word, we can be taken advantage of by every circumstance that throws itself at us. There is a darkness that comes because of ignorance. When we became a Christian, the Lord wants to deliver us from two things: the first was sin and the second was stupidity. Some people keep making the same mistake again and again and again. If we neglect to get wisdom from the Word, if we neglect to get wisdom from life, we are like a dog that keeps on returning to its own vomit.[99] There is a whole whack of scriptures about renewing your mind[100] and "girding up the loins" of our mind; we need to apply these truths to our thinking.

Demonic attack

Darkness is produced by a demonic attack upon our lives. Ephesians 6 talks about the *evil day*, which is not a 24- hour period. It could be a season—an hour, a day, a month, a year— where demonic powers are trying to discourage us, dishearten us, tell us to give up, to quit, to go back to our old lives. The Bible says there is a darkness that is produced because of a demonic attack upon our lives. The Bible says, *"So put on all the armour that God gives. Then when that evil day comes, you will be able to defend yourself. And when the* battle is over, you will still be standing firm."[101]

Divine Darkness

There is a fourth kind of darkness—I threw in the first three for free—and I want to spend most of this chapter discussing this particular type of darkness. I would like to consider the divine darkness. This is the kind of darkness the text at the beginning of the chapter refers to. What happens when God turns the light out? What happens when there is the removal of the conscious presence of God in our lives? If you have not had this experience, let me prophesy, it is coming. If you have already had this experience, let me prophesy, it is coming again.

That is not very encouraging teaching, I know. It is especially discouraging if you do not know what is happening or why. That is why I want to explain this to you. I have experienced seasons of the divine darkness; it is almost uncanny how it comes.

You can be sitting in church singing all your favourite songs, but there is no feeling of divine activity going on inside of your body. You may think, "Wow! The Bible says if I have something against somebody then I should go and apologise." So you start apologising to people you have never even met and the darkness is still on you. Then you think, "I need a serious time of prayer." So, you get up three minutes earlier than you normally would and have a real serious time of prayer. Still nothing. You wrack your brains and think, "I know what is wrong. It is the devil." So you rebuke the devil, you curse the devil, you plead the blood, you walk around the house with a cross on your head engaging in spiritual warfare, and still no change. You are rapidly running out of options. You think, "My gosh, I probably need to go to a meeting and have a healing of memories. Or maybe one of my legs is shorter than the other." Still no change. The consciousness of the presence of Jesus is no longer there.

I have a friend who has done a lot of university work in the States. On one occasion, he spoke at a Christian university. As he was about to go up on the stage, a 19-year-old woman grabbed him by the hand and said, "Are you the lecturer?" He said, "Yes, I am." She said, "Are you as stupid as all the other Christians in this college?" He responded, "Well, I do not know. What is your problem?" She had a legal pad full of questions that she had posed to professors but apparently had not received satisfactory answers. He said, "I can't answer all of these right now, but throw one at me and I'll have a go." She said, "Do Christians follow Jesus Christ just because of the good feelings they get?"

Now, that is a bit of a nasty question, because, to be honest with you, Jesus gives me nice feelings. He gives me joy, He gives me peace, and He gives me an inner feeling of security that everything is going to be all right. That young woman asked a very penetrating question. We do not serve Jesus just because of the by-products. We serve Jesus because He is God of the whole universe. He has demanded our lives and we have resolutely, unreservedly given our lives to Him. The by-products of the commitment are love, joy, peace, the indwelling Holy Spirit, blessing, prosperity, goodness, abundance, kindness, and all the wonderful things that happen to us.

But when the light goes out, we find out what our motivation is for being a Christian. Five tests occur when the light goes out.

The Test of Courage

One of the first tests is the test of courage. You need courage to walk in the darkness. Remember when you were a little kid, and you needed the light on at night? When the light is on, and the joy of the Lord is your strength, and everything that you do is blessed, and you are succeeding and prospering, and the kids are happy, it is fantastic. You do not need much courage then.

You need courage when the light goes off: when chaos breaks out, when you are sowing but not reaping, when you are praying and there is no answer, when you are witnessing and no one is being saved. Worse still, there is no consciousness of the presence of Jesus. I believe no wimps get to heaven. I think it takes incredible courage to be a Christian. I think courage is a Christian virtue.

The Test of Convictions

The second test is the test of our convictions. It is fantastic to believe in divine healing when you are not sick. It is a little more challenging when you feel a migraine coming on. What do you do first? Grab the pill bottle or talk to Dr. Jesus? I remember having tonsillitis. I had had two or three doses of penicillin, but it was not shifting. I was sweating like a pig, groggy and wiped out. I was getting irritated because I had done everything and nothing was changing. Then I decided to pray. I guess I am a bit slow. I laid my hands on my greasy sweating head and said, "Jesus, I have flippin' had enough. I have flippin' had enough! Rebuke this thing!" Within an hour and a half, the fever lifted off me and I got out of bed. I had not been out of bed for 3 weeks. When you have been sick for a long time, when numerous people have prayed for you and nothing has happened your conviction on divine healing is tested.

Have you ever been unemployed? Your conviction about tithing can get a bit thin when you are out of work. "Come, Lord, let us reason together. I need a break!" One of my first faith experiences happened when I went off to Bible College. It was huge for me. I was being encouraged by everyone from my home church, but none of the encouragement was monetary.

"It will be alright, Ian," they would say as they drove away in their Jaguar. I had worked for eight months before I went to college and had managed to save my first three months' tuition. Two months before college began, Jesus said to me, "I want you to give that money away." I rebuked that demon in the name of Jesus because that could not possibly be right. I heard the voice again, "I want you to give it." This time I knew it was definitely the Lord, so I gave the money away. I now had no money. Do you understand what no money means? It means NO MONEY. As an aside, I understood nothing at this point in my life about the scriptural principles of giving, or about sowing and reaping.

The church held a small farewell for me during the Sunday night service just before college, and they gave me a gift! I was sure they were going to pay my fees. Instead, they gave me an absolutely ridiculous gift; they gave me a Bible. I was thinking, "Flippin' heck, what are they giving a Bible for? I am going to *Bible* College; there must be hundreds of Bibles in the Bible College. I do not need a Bible; I need cash." I remember thinking, "I won't even be able to sell it. There'll be an oversupply and I'll get nothing for it." After the service, I remember walking to the car of the friend who was driving me to the college the next day. I still had no money.

I was thinking, "Tomorrow morning I am going to arrive at the Bible College and they will want three months' fees in advance. Jesus should have turned up by now."

When you get that desperate, you imagine anything can happen. I was looking for angels to appear. I was expecting Jesus to plant money in my pocket. I was just climbing into the car when somebody came running across the church car park. They put a thick, brown, holy envelope in my hand. It felt holy because I could feel the bank notes. I was so excited I ran back into the church, went to the loo, and ripped it open. It was my first semester fees. That was lucky wasn't it? No, that was Jesus.

The Test of Consecration

A third test that comes to us is a test of consecration. When the joy of the Lord is our strength, we can resist those fiery darts of the devil because the shield of faith is in place. When the light goes off and you do not feel any momentum, any presence of Jesus, it is easy to compromise our faith. We can engage in conversations that are a little too near the bone. They are a bit dodgy—maybe sexual innuendoes, or gossip or tittle-tattle. We give up our righteousness for a laugh. We surrender our holiness to impress someone. When the light goes off, it takes commitment, it takes strength to hold to what is true and wholesome and pure and lovely. I did not get married until I was

34 years of age. I could not find anybody willing to take the risk. Fathers were hiding their daughters from me. When I was 20 years of age, I did not believe that any Christian could have a sexual problem. I believed that because I was convinced that I had everybody's sexual hormones in *my* body. So how could *they* possibly have a problem?

I had flown to Australia for the first time in 1989. I had spoken at a conference and several other places when several airlines went on strike. I was in Melbourne and my departing flight was in Brisbane—which was a heck of a walk, about 2000 miles.

Through some jiggery-pokery, I found an international carrier that would get me to my destination. This was the icing on the cake as I had come to Australia from India where I had 54 meetings in 17 days. After being on the road for five and a half weeks, I was absolutely knicky-knacky, I was thrashed. I could not wait to get back home.

I had eight hours to kill before my flight to London. I walked around the shops, bought a newspaper, which I read back to front. This took all of 20 minutes. I was sitting in the airport when this little thought came into my mind, "Nobody knows that you are here. All your friends live in the north part of the city and the airport is in the south part of the city. You could do anything. Who is ever going to find out?" I am tired. I am 33 years of age. I am a man. I have sexual desires. The voice echoed again, "You could go down into the city, who is ever going to know?" I got in line to buy a bus ticket to go down to the city, because I had another seven hours left. I was about two people from the front of the line when a loud voice in my spirit said, "WHAT DO YOU THINK YOU ARE DOING? ARE YOU STUPID OR WHAT?" I had a flippin' heart attack. I got out of the line, picked up my briefcase and started walking up and down. I started speaking in tongues, I read my Bible, and I did everything I could to come against this thing. But do you know what?

It was not moving. It took an hour and three quarters to blast that temptation out of my spirit. When the light goes off, you are vulnerable. Darkness is a test of commitment to the most precious parts of your Christian life.

The Test of Our Calling

A fourth test that comes during a time of darkness is the test of our calling. You ask yourself, "Why am I doing this?" The temptation is to have a pity party and feel sorry for yourself. This test comes to our lives because Jesus is trying to get us to discover why we are serving Him.

It is a privilege to serve Jesus. As a new Christian, I answered the call to put a Christian leaflet in every door in my town. I did not think that was hard work. It was a privilege. I was happy to be on the cleaning team of my church, do the dishes, clean the windows, and even clean the loo. "What an honour, I can serve Jesus!" However, when the light goes out, we discover who we are serving and why. Are we serving Jesus for the by-products or for Jesus Himself?

In my first youth pastorate, I was to preach the next Sunday. I tried for three or four days to get a message, but nothing came. I had files of lecture notes, illustrations and jokes. I knew how to put a message together, but I was completely blank. In desperation, I rang the senior pastor on the phone Saturday at midnight and said, "I can't do it tomorrow morning."

He said, "You what? It is 12:00 o'clock and you are telling me you can't do it for the 10:00 a.m. service?" I said, "Mate, I am sorry, I can't do it."

I got to the church Sunday morning, and, of course, my

name was in the bulletin and everyone was expecting me to preach. I somehow got through the worship time. Then, we began to have communion. I was feeling so gross, and I prayed in my spirit, "God, I do not want to be where I am right now. I do not want to be in this experience." Do you know what Jesus said to me? He said, "Do you love Me? Do you love Me more than preaching? Than leading? Than the respect the people give you? How much do you love Me?" When the light goes off, we actually find out why we are serving Jesus.

The Test of Our Conversion

The last test is the test of our conversion experience. Have you ever doubted if you have been born again? I have. I began to have thoughts like this: "How old was I? Yeah, I was 14. Well, you are pretty vulnerable at 14. I probably went through a religious, emotional experience. I made a decision that I am probably growing out of." A time of spiritual darkness often causes us to doubt our salvation. Wisdom teaches us to doubt our doubts. We have to learn to doubt our doubts. Romans chapter eight is there to teach us how to be certain that we are the children of God. It tells us that we can be one hundred per cent certain of our salvation. *I am sure that nothing can separate us from God's love-not life or death, not angels or spirits, not the present or the future, and not powers above or powers below. Nothing in all creation can separate us from God's love for us in Christ Jesus our Lord!*[102]

God wants to put greater substance in our lives because Christianity is more than a whack of throwaway phrases and clichés. "Oh, come on brother, just praise the Lord." Yeah, well, you try praising the Lord when the light is off. God wants to produce Christ-like faith and character in our lives. Like Jesus, we may face our own Garden of Gethsemane experience where the presence of God seems a million miles away.

When God turns the light off, He is trying to produce greater levels of substance and faith in our lives. Some of the most incredible experiences of church history occurred when the lights went out.

In this chapter, we have seen that spiritual darkness tests our courage, our convictions, our consecration, our calling and our conversion. It is vital that we heed the warning of scripture. *But watch out, you who live in your own light and warm yourselves by your own fire, this reward you shall receive from me: you will lie down in great torment.*[103]

In next chapter, I want to show you how to respond to periods of darkness.

Faith to Walk in Darkness: Study Guide

Flight Plan

The enemy has lots of tactics that he wants to use to derail and sabotage our faith; lies, sin and direct assault on us. Some of these things we open the door to by the choices we make and Satan being the legalist he is, certainly take every opportunity we give him. However, the "whats's" still happen as we live in a fallen world, and many of these are situations far beyond our control. God uses these situations to reveal our hearts and reveal himself. He uses them to shape and prune us. He uses them to reveal to us the power and anointing he has placed in us and how to use it for his Kingdom purposes. These chapters of "divine darkness" often become tests that God allows us to walk through, and as some have said. With God, often the test comes first and the lesson follows. Some tests we may encounter could be:

Test of courage

Test of convictions

Test of consecration

Test of our calling

Test of our conversion

Do you recognise one or more of these tests in your history with God? What did you learn about your own identity? What did you learn about the nature of God? Ponder on these quotes from the chapter before you move on and allow the Holy Spirit to whisper to you:

"But when the light goes out, we find out what our motivation is for being a Christian."

"We give up our righteousness for a laugh. We surrender our holiness to impress someone."

"When God turns the light off, He is trying to produce greater levels of substance and faith in our lives."

Take-Off

In this chapter Ian shared about his college experience.

He felt he was supposed to go and worked hard to save the first three months of tuition. Just before school Jesus asks him to give away all that he worked for, seemingly making it impossible for him to pay for the school year he felt was obedience in the first place.

He found himself asking the question the day before school was to start, "Jesus should have turned up by now." Have you ever had this moment? Or perhaps like most of us, we don't get to that moment because we won't give away the money in the first place – it is not logical! We don't put ourselves in a place where God has to show up or else. We cover our own bases, you know, in case God fails. These moments expose our lack of faith which we either repent for and embrace the pruning, or we justify and step back from the ledge of big faith in God.

If these tests haven't come, don't worry, they will, and as much as you try to prepare yourself it will be harder than you want it to be. There is risk involved. If there isn't, it's likely not faith you are walking in. In this chapter we discovered some of the tests that God wants us to pass. This helps us recognise the season and recalibrate to respond in faith. To do this however, we need to be honest with ourselves and with God about where we are at. Will you dare to bare it all for the sake of growing your faith?

Is there anything you aren't willing to put on the table before God?

Flight Crew

Discussion Questions:

1) What season of divine darkness resonates with you the most? Share. (Test of courage, convictions, consecration, calling and conversion.)

2) In the past have you recognised the times when you have faced "testing" – while you were in it? Why or why not?

3) What mindset do we need to have to prepare and help us succeed for seasons of divine darkness?

4) What role do others in the body of Christ play in this?

5) What role does our own understanding of ourselves and our identity in Christ play in this?

6) What role does knowing the truth of who God is, play in this?

Captain's Log

Reflection: "Not everything that is faced can be changed, but nothing can be changed until it is faced." James Baldwin. What are some areas in your life that you have avoided facing? What has it cost you? What is possible when you gain victory?

Journal Prompt: Walk through and journal with Holy Spirit to see what needs to be faced in your life right now and ask Holy Spirit to give you next steps. Tackle one each day for the next week:

Day 1 Sin – Is there sin I refuse to deal with in my life? Is there an area of my life I have failed to take responsibility to change – I am aware of it, but keep repeating it?

Day 2 Demonic Attack – Is the enemy attacking? Have I applied all of the armour of God?

Day 3 Test of courage: Is there any area of your life where fear wins over courage?

Day 4 Test of convictions: Is there any area of your life where your talk does not match your walk?

Day 5 Test of consecration: Is there any area of my life where compromise is permitted or even habitual?

Day 6 Test of our calling: Can you see any self-serving motivations that Holy Spirit wants you to deal with?

Day 7 Test of our conversion: Where does a lie about your conversion keep a door open to doubt in your life?

In-Flight Training

Journaling is a significant part of reflecting and sorting out what is going on inside of us. Prioritise your journaling habit this week.

1) Journal & reflect daily with Holy Spirit.
2) Repent and consecrate yourself afresh to God.
3) Ask God to show you truth to stand on.
4) Ask God for an action step – something to practice, a step of obedience to take.
5) Practice it daily until it becomes habit.

Checking IN or Checking OUT?

Take a moment to listen to your inner dialogue as you consider the commitments you are making. What temptations to "check out" of these commitments do you see? What justification creeps in that allows you not to take this too seriously? What hurry, worry or fear knocks at the door? What power do you have available to you to deal with these enemy tactics? What will you choose when they confront you this week?

Will you check IN or check OUT?

Ground Control

Set some time aside for silence and solitude. Invite your heavenly Father to speak to you by His Holy Spirit. What thoughts bubble up? What is the still small voice whispering to you?

1) Write it down.
2) Test it. (Is it congruent with the nature of God and with scripture?)
3) Make it sacred; do not dismiss it, but take it seriously.

Soaring Higher

God is trying to produce Godly character in us. Read Gal 5:22-25 Score yourself from 1-10 (1 – Non-existent, 10 a Habitual part of your character) on each of the 9 fruits of the spirit. What areas is holy Spirit highlighting to you as opportunities to press into Godly Character more? Allow him to speak to you about what happens if you ignore these areas.

You need courage when the lights go off;

What to Do When Darkness Falls

"Darkness cannot drive out darkness: only light can do that.

Hate cannot drive out hate: only love can do that."[104]

— Martin Luther King Jr.

"Who among you fears the Lord and obeys the word of his servant? If you are walking in the darkness, without a ray of light, trust in the name of the Lord and rely on your God.

But watch out, you who live in your own light and warm yourselves by your own fire, this reward you shall receive from me: you will lie down in great torment."[105]

In this chapter, I want to continue to explore what to do when God turns off the lights. The first thing we need to understand is that if God has turned out the lights, only God can turn them back on. There is nothing you can do. The light switch is in heaven. The text does warn of a human response to divine darkness: you can turn on your *own light* or *warm yourselves by your own fire*. The result is not very pleasant: *"you will lie down in great torment."*

When God has turned off the light, it is off for specific reasons. He wants to spotlight some needed character formation, challenge some attitudes and test your courage. We outlined the tests in the previous chapter. However, there are things we can do.

Walk

The Biblical passage we are considering is Isaiah 50:10. Verse 10 says, *"If you are* walking *in the darkness...."* Walking does not mean just being out for a stroll. It is not a zombie-like existence. Walking, to use the New Testament analogy, means doing what is right even if you do not like it. You just do it. It is a matter of disciplined obedience.

When the lights go off, you probably will not want to read

the Bible. In fact, you will probably think that the back panel on the cereal box is far more interesting than the Bible. But do not give in to that. You have to get the Word inside you, because *"People reap what they sow."* [106] If you put the Word into the darkness, it cannot do anything but produce light. *"Your word is a lamp to my feet and a light for my path."* [107] You may not want to read it, but read it just the same. You will want to avoid church. It is easy to think, "I am not going to *that* church. They are all a bunch of hypocrites." We can be critical of the music, the preaching, the ushers or the colour of the carpet. A critical spirit knows no boundaries. We have to grab that attitude by the throat and wrestle it into submission. I have learned that when I do not want to come to church, whatever happens, come hell or high water, I have to get to the house of God. The church is Christ's Body, and if there is one place I can go to find light, it is the church of the Living God.

You may not feel like praying. You will feel your prayers are hitting an iron ceiling and bouncing back on your noggin. That is not a good feeling, but you have to press through, you have to keep walking.

The Bible says, *"Call to me and I will answer you..."* [108]

Jesus said, *"Keep on asking, and you will receive what you ask for. Keep on seeking, and you will find. Keep on knocking, and the door will be opened to you. For everyone who asks, receives. Everyone who seeks, finds. And to everyone who knocks, the door will be opened."* [109] Those in darkness must walk.

Trust in the Name of the Lord

The second thing our text tells us is, *"Trust in the name of the Lord."* When the light is off, it is hard to trust in Jesus because He seems very distant. He feels a billion miles away, but He says, "I want you to trust in the name of the Lord." He wants us to trust *the name*, the covenant name of God. You do not trust in your feelings or circumstances. You trust in God's name. There are seven primary covenant names of God. These names are light-giving as well as life-giving.

Jehovah- Jireh means God is my provider. When the light is turned off, when our resources have dried up, we trust in the name Jehovah-Jireh. Tell God you agree with His Word and His Name and that you trust in His provision. [110]

Jehovah-Shalom means God is my peace. We can feel

tossed around by life and by circumstances. Take the peace of God into the centre of your being. He is Jehovah Shalom. *"Do not be anxious about anything, but in everything, by prayer and petition, with thanksgiving, present your requests to God. And the peace of God, which transcends all understanding, will guard your hearts and your minds in Christ Jesus."*[111]

Jehovah-Shammah means the Lord is there. Perhaps you do not feel Him, there is no visible evidence of His presence, or prayer does not seem to work, but He IS there. He is *right there*, not a billion miles away. You see, God is the greatest person of substance in the whole universe. Physics tell us nothing is solid. Your kitchen table feels solid, but physics tells us nothing is solid. That table is made up of millions of molecules that are constantly changing and moving. It looks solid to the naked eye, but it is not. God is solid. He is immutable, unchangeable, the most permanent substance in the whole universe.

C.S. Lewis was a profound Christian philosopher in England. He lectured at both Oxford and Cambridge Universities. He said to his students one day, "When Jesus appeared to His disciples and He came in through the wall, did He come through the wall because He was less dense or denser than the wall?"

Every molecule in that brick wall recognised its creator. It is as if the bricks were saying, "If the creator wanted to get in, we'll move out of the way." In He came. Jesus is more concrete and has more substance than a solid brick wall.

Faith is not something you hold on to; faith is something that holds you. Lean on God; learn to rely on the name of God. The other four covenant names of God are as follows. **Jehovah-Tsidkenu** means the Lord is my righteousness, my sure salvation.[112] **Jehovah-Nissi** means the Lord is my banner of victory, my sure deliverance over the enemy.[113] **Jehovah-Rophe** means the Lord is my healer.[114] **Jehovah-M'Kaddesh** means the Lord who sanctifies, or the Lord who sets me apart for wholeness.[115]

Most parents of small children have played this game, especially with a little tyke who is learning to swim. The parent steps back a pace and says, "Come on, jump!" The child jumps and the parent catches them before their head goes under. Then you step back another pace and do it again. Then you step back four paces and encourage another bold leap. This time you let the child belly flop into the water. When their little head emerges, the child is coughing and spluttering. You take them to the side of the pool and say, "I want to teach you a very important lesson; you can't trust anyone in this life." Of course, you would not really do that, unless you were a horrible parent. Nevertheless, life has done that to us from time to time. We can end up projecting that same lack of trust on the Lord. Nevertheless, Jesus says, "I want you to lean on Me." You cannot see Him, but if you lean far enough, you hit substance. "I want you to rely on Me."

Personal Benefits

How do we receive the benefits that God intends from a period of personal spiritual darkness? First, recognise what is happening. Second, discern what the tests are that God is allowing in your life. Third, keep living life while learning to trust in the name of the Lord. Walking through darkness will develop spiritual sinew in your life. You will end up with a faith that brings glory to God. You will not have a second hand faith; you will have a personalised faith. It will not be a preacher's story from the platform or a carbon copy of the faith of your parents or mentors; you will actually have your own story. That is the first benefit. You will have your own miracle testimony of God working in your life.

The second benefit that will come to your life is humility. Sometimes we become proud of the information that we accumulate. Instead of being a tool, knowledge has become a badge. "I know more than you." When we go through the dark valley, we become broken. We no longer think we are better than other people. We are no longer puffed up with our own spiritual pride.

We learn to embrace pain. We live in a world that does not like pain. We try to eradicate pain as quickly as possible. You can get a pill, a fortified super strength Tylenol or Advil, to deal with the pain. In the Christian life, however, we must to learn to embrace pain. Pain is one of the tools God uses to make us into the people we need to be. We are pushing away pain, difficult circumstances and difficult people. But God is up to something and we are not getting it. We have to see Jesus in the middle of our pain and ask, "OK Jesus, what's the deal?" The pain can last 11 days or the pain can last 40 years—you cast the vote. When the children of Israel left Egypt for the Promised Land, they could have made the journey in 11 days. But the 11-day journey took them 40 years. Why? They kept avoiding the pain. But what happened? They had more pain, more pain than they could imagine. But they did not get it, they did not learn the lesson.

When the light goes out, we need to adopt a posture of humility.

Third, God gives us a heart for lost people. Sometimes we forget what it was to be lost. I did not grow up in a Christian family, so I remember clearly the feeling of being lost. I remember at 14 years of age lying on my bed thinking, "What the... is this all about?" I was in turmoil trying to find my identity. I did not know what to do with my life. We tend to forget what is was like when we came to Jesus. We want to forget it because that is the ugly past. When the light goes off, we remember how lost people feel and think. We develop a concern, a heart and a passion for the lost. We feel the pain of a hurting person in our workplace. We feel the loneliness of people sitting by themselves in restaurants. A transaction takes place in our spirit; we receive a new revelation of the love of Christ.

Fourth, you will learn to pray like you have never prayed before. You will prove the power of prayer. Remember the story of Jonah? He thought that he had pulled the wrong straw, but he had pulled the right straw. He said to the crew of the beleaguered ship, "I am your man. Throw me over and everything will be OK." So they threw him into the sea and he was swallowed by a large fish. He was in the belly of the fish—talk about a time of darkness! Jonah was thinking, "OK, I blew it. I have sinned. If you just get me out of this mess I'll do whatever you want."

He prayed but nothing happened. Then he had an intense breakthrough in prayer and the fish had the worst stomach-ache of its life and spewed him out on the beach. We discover the depths of prayer in the valley, not on the mountaintop. We find God when we wrestle some issue to the ground, as Jacob wrestled with God. When the light goes out, we are less casual about prayer. Prayer is no longer a spare wheel – it becomes the steering wheel!

Finally, you will come back into the light. God decides when to turn the light back on. It is determined by His will. You do not know when, but He will. If you have had the opportunity to travel through the Alps, you have discovered there are long tunnels that go through mountains. Sometimes the tunnels are 5 km long. During the summer, you drive from bright sunshine into the subdued lighting of the tunnel. As you drive through the tunnel, your eyes begin to relax and your pupils grow larger as they hunt for more light. When you come out the other side, whoosh, the light hits you and, suddenly, everything takes on incredible definition. The greens look greener; the sky looks bluer than you have ever seen it. When we emerge from spiritual darkness, we see Jesus in a fresh way: the grace of God is richer and the peace of God is profound.

Many people have experienced this darkness and, like me, they did not have a clue what was going on. The Puritans in England called this the *dark night of the soul*. It feels like that. However, we do come out. But I have to respect the text. If we decide to light our own fires, try to escape what God is doing, try to find a shortcut, we will end up lying down in torment. Things *will* get worse. We need tenacious faith to walk in the darkness; it is a challenging season. Yet, it is one of the most profound deposits of grace that God makes in our lives.

What to Do When Darkness Falls: Study Guide

Flight Plan

We walk into this next chapter understanding that God uses divine darkness to expel darkness from inside of us and to purify our ambitions, affections and motivations. Learning how to respond well in these seasons in our life needs to become habit and lifestyle. Learning to trust in the name of the Lord is key. To this, we must come to a place of increasing understanding of who he is and how he is described in scripture so we can grow in faith and confidence. Consider these quotes:

"If you put the word in the darkness, it cannot do anything but produce light."

"Those in darkness must walk."

"But the 11-day journey took them 40 years. Why? They kept avoiding the pain."

Take-Off

In this chapter we looked at some of the names of God and how holding to the truth of these becomes light in the darkness for us. However, let's explore more intently why this is important. First of all, scripture says that "The name of the Lord is a strong fortress; the godly run to him and are safe." Proverbs 18:10. There is power in the name of the Lord. Read Exodus 20:1-7 the first 3 of 10 Commandments and take time on your own or in a group to go through the Flight Crew group discussions to explore the connection between God's law and his name.

Flight Crew

Discussion Questions:

1) Vs 7 Says "do not misuse the name of the Lord". What does this mean?

2) Most common interpretation is "don't use God's name to swear" does this seem petty in light of the surrounding commands? What could a deeper meaning be?

3) Brian Beattie a good friend of Ian says this regarding this scripture: "I think it's a better interpretation to

believe that "taking God's name in vain" happens when we don't <u>believe</u> who He says He is." Believe, faith and trust are synonymous in the Hebrew scripture. What are the implications of this?

4) There are many "names of God" in scripture including ones noted on pages 303-305. Which ones are hard for you to hold fast to as true?

Captain's Log

<u>Reflection:</u> There are many "names of God" in scripture including the seven noted on pages 303-305. What stands out to you from this list? Why?

<u>Journal Prompt:</u> Each day take one of the names of God and complete the questions below:

1) Do I believe that God is _____?
2) Why does it matter that I believe this?
3) How change does this truth require in my thoughts, attitudes and actions?
4) What is Holy Spirit saying to me about this?
5) What decision do I need to make about my future!

In-Flight Training

"Those in darkness must walk"

"If you're going through hell, keep going"

1) Do you see hopelessness creeping in? Is it still worth the price?

2) What actions can you take to arrest this from what you have learned in this chapter?

3) What will you do?

4) When will you do it!

Checking IN or Checking OUT?

Take a moment to listen to your inner dialogue as you consider the commitments you are making. What temptations to "check out" of these commitments do you see? What justification creeps in that allows you not to take this too seriously? What hurry, worry or fear knocks at the door? What power do you have available to you to deal with these enemy tactics? What will you choose when they confront you this week?

Will you check IN or check OUT?

Ground Control

Set some time aside for silence and solitude. Invite your heavenly Father to speak to you by His Holy Spirit. What thoughts bubble up? What is the still small voice whispering to you?

1) Write it down.

2) Test it. (Is it congruent with the nature of God and with scripture?)

3) Make it sacred; do not dismiss it, but take it seriously.

Soaring Higher

Research more of the names of God – what do they tell you about who God is and who you are becoming as one made in His image?

We need tenacious faith to walk in the darkness, it is a challenging season. Yet it is one of the most profound deposits of grace that God makes in our lives.

Hearing the Voice of God

. "Hearing God is not all that difficult. If we know the Lord, we have already heard His voice - after all it was the inner leading that brought us to Him in the first place. But we can hear His voice and still miss His best if we don't keep on listening. After the what of guidance comes the when and how."[116]

- Loren Cunningham

How do we hear God's voice? How do we know if it is the voice of the Lord? How do we know it is not just our imagination? How do we know it is not the devil? How do we know it is not the flesh? The Bible has clear principles to help us discern the origin and distinguish the message of the voices speaking to us. We are going to discover some principles in the well-known passage from 1 Kings 19.

There [Elijah] came to a cave, where he spent the night. But the LORD said to him, "What are you doing here, Elijah?" Elijah replied, "I have zealously served the LORD God Almighty. But the people of Israel have broken their covenant with you, torn down your altars, and killed every one of your prophets. I am the only one left, and now they are trying to kill me, too."

"Go out and stand before me on the mountain," the LORD told him. And as Elijah stood there, the LORD passed by, and a mighty windstorm hit the mountain. It was such a terrible blast that the rocks were torn loose, but the LORD was not in the wind. After the wind there was an earthquake, but the LORD was not in the earthquake. And after the earthquake there was a fire, but the LORD was not in the fire. And after the fire there was the sound of a gentle whisper. When Elijah heard it, he wrapped his face in his cloak and went out and stood at the entrance of the cave. And a voice said, "What are you doing here, Elijah?" He replied again, "I have zealously served the LORD God Almighty. But the people of Israel have broken their covenant with you, torn down your altars, and killed every one of your prophets. I am the only one left, and now they are trying to kill me, too." Then the LORD told him, "Go back the same way you came, and travel to the wilderness of Damascus. When you arrive there, anoint Hazael to be king of

Aram. Then anoint Jehu son of Nimshi to be king of Israel, and anoint Elisha son of Shaphat from the town of Abel-meholah to replace you as my prophet. Anyone who escapes from Hazael will be killed by Jehu, and those who escape Jehu will be killed by Elisha! Yet I will preserve 7,000 others in Israel who have never bowed down to Baal or kissed him!"[117] I also want to mention two verses from the New Testament.

"Anyone whose father is God listens gladly to the words of God. Since you do not, it proves you are not God's children"[118]

"My sheep recognise my voice and I know them and they follow me."[119]

It is imperative that we begin to understand how to hear the voice of God. It is part of our inheritance. Jesus said in John 10, *"My sheep hear my voice."* Many times, we hear the voice of God but we do not know how to distinguish the other voices speaking to us. We need clarification in this regard.

Two Extremes

The Old Testament employs dramatic language when it says, *"The word of the Lord came"* to such and such a prophet. We need to be aware of two extremes. We can think, "Well, I am not a prophet of God. I cannot hear the voice of God like those men in the Old Testament. I am just a little Christian." Yet, the New Testament teaches that we are the children of God and that God loves to communicate to us. The one extreme is that we are not good enough, holy enough or wise enough. The other extreme is, "Unless I have cloud formations with skywriting and the smiling face of Jesus, I am not going to believe what God has said to me." Let us find a place of balance.

Supernaturally Normal

When you became a Christian, you were inducted into the supernatural Body of Christ[120] and became a partaker of the divine nature.[121] First Corinthians says you were baptized into His Body[122]. You had a supernatural immersion that made you acutely aware of the supernatural.[123] People have different spiritual experiences; for some it is dramatic, for others it is more subtle.

The moment I received the baptism of the Holy Spirit, it seemed as if worlds opened up to me. I became sensitive and conscious of the supernatural, something I had not been aware of before.

It is utterly normal for Christians to operate in the

supernatural. It is abnormal not to, because we are supernatural beings. We have been brought from death to life.[124] We have the Spirit of Christ inside of us.[125] The spirit man inside of us longs to communicate with our Heavenly Father: our spirit with His Spirit.[126] All of that is completely normal.

Tuning Your Ear to Hear

In the story told above, Elijah was told to take his position on the mountain because the Lord was going to appear. Through this story, we discover four ways in which God communicated, though He *spoke* through only one. Elijah's experience is not unique. God has used all four of these methods on other occasions. The issue for us is to discern between the way that God gets our attention and the way in which He speaks.

As Elijah stood waiting, a wind came and ripped up the rocks. It was not unusual for God to communicate in that way. In Ezekiel, the purposes of God came out of a whirling wind. On the day of Pentecost, the outpouring of the Holy Spirit was announced by the sound of a mighty rushing wind. The wind was the not voice of God, it was more of an announcement or a precursor of the purposes of God.

Then there was an earthquake. God had broadcast His purposes that way before. The mountains shook when Moses received the Law.[127] There was an earthquake when Jesus rose from the dead, signalling He was alive and well.[128] God has worked through earthquakes, but on this occasion, He was not speaking through the earthquake.

There had also been Divine communication through fire. A pillar of fire led the children of Israel by night as a clear means of God's guidance.[129] On Mount Carmel Elijah prayed, and God confirmed that He was the true and living God by sending fire from heaven to consume the sacrifice.[130] God had worked through fire before, but on this occasion, He was not speaking through the fire.

Finally, after the roaring of the elements and the shaking of the mountain, a gentle whisper. God spoke to Elijah through a still small voice. He had communicated in this way with Adam and Eve in the Garden of Eden.[131] The wind, fire and earthquake were convincing demonstrations of the presence of the Lord—that He was passing by. Then, the quiet voice of God speaking to the broken and discouraged prophet. The cacophony of the elements followed by a gentle whisper.

Some people say that unless they have three pieces of scripture, nine cloud formations and 15 fleeces, they have not heard the voice of God. If that is the case, we have missed the point. The point is to hear the voice of God, to understand it, and then to obey it. God does not always speak in the way that we might think. Elijah was looking for comfort; instead, he got a question followed by a command. God may not always say what we want Him to say, but He always says what we need to hear.

How God Speaks

Essentially, the still small voice of God is His spirit speaking to our spirit. In 1 Corinthians 2:14 it says, *"The natural man receives not the things of the spirit of God, for they are foolishness to him, and he cannot understand them, because they are spiritually discerned."* Job 32:8 says, *"There is a spirit in man and the Lord gives him understanding."* Romans 8:16 says, *"The Spirit himself testifies with our spirit that we are God's children."*

The Holy Spirit speaks to the believer's spirit.[132] It is almost never an audible voice; it is a quiet voice heard in the heart by the ear of the spirit.

Some people, who have had dramatic guidance in the past, feel that unless they get something equally as dramatic, they are not hearing from God. That is a dangerous way to think and can make one prey to false guidance from the world, the flesh or the devil. It is not *how* God speaks—dreams, visions, thunder or lightning—it is the means by *which* He speaks. He speaks through the gentle voice of His Spirit.

Misconceptions

Let us look at three misconceptions about hearing the voice of God. They include, misuse of the Bible, the Fleecing Game, and the Medium Effect.

Misuse of the Bible

The first misconception is the misuse of the Bible. We are all familiar with *finger-guidance*: placing one's finger at random in the Bible, possibly with closed eyes, and saying, "God, talk to me." If it is not a good message, we do it again. I would like to suggest to you that is an illegitimate and unreliable way to seek guidance. A curious example of this practice is John Wesley. He often resorted to casting lots or opening his Bible at random to receive guidance. On one occasion, he was looking for guidance as to whether he should go to Bristol to preach to thousands that had been gathered by the ministry of his friend George Whitefield. Four times he "consulted the oracle" and each time the verses he lighted upon referred to death or suffering. F*inger-guidance* led him to believe that if he went to Bristol, he would die. His brother Charles had the same fate confirmed by Scripture.

Nevertheless, John bravely went to Bristol accompanied by Charles who "desired to die with him." Yet all these forebodings were entirely unnecessary. In going to Bristol, instead of approaching his death, John Wesley was entering into the most fruitful labour of his life.[133] And he lived five decades longer.

Sometimes we look for verses to agree with our viewpoint. This is called proof-texting. This is also a bad way to seek God's guidance. Someone once said the Bible was written to show us the sort of people we are to be, so God can show us the places He wants us to go, and not the other way around. If our character is in line with Jesus, you can be sure He is going to speak to us. I have had confirmation from the scriptures of things that God told me to do and I have gone with that. I have had promises given to me that have been in line with what God has already said.

The Bible says a cord of three strands is not easily broken.[134] I have found that for critical guidance, for big life decisions, it's good to get confirmation from three sources; a virtual three-stranded cord.

Rather than proof-texting, I would encourage you to ask God for confirmation through some combination of the following: an opening door of opportunity, agreeing words of guidance, the peace of God, a scriptural truth, or the voice of the Spirit speaking to your heart or spirit.

The Fleecing Game

A second misuse is the Fleecing Game. This is another incorrect way to receive guidance, and yet it is accepted in Pentecostal circles. Let me give you five reasons why I believe it is an incorrect means of guidance. The context of setting out a fleece is in Judges chapter 6. Gideon said to the Lord, "If you make the fleece dry and the ground wet, then I know I am to be your man." When the Lord did it, he still was not sure, so he asked God to reverse the process.

Here are five reasons why this is a misapplied and misused form of determining God's guidance. First, nowhere in the New Testament do you find men of the Spirit using fleeces. Second, fleeces often need the cooperation of others who may not be obedient to God. Third, it is a lack of faith. What we are actually saying is that the voice of God is not enough.

Gideon was declaring his unbelief in the verbal guidance of God by asking for confirmation via the fleece. The Bible says, *"Whatsoever is not of faith, is sin."* [135] When we put out a fleece, we are actually asking God to bless unbelief, which is sin. How bizarre is that? Fourth, fleecing makes the obvious ridiculous. A man once said to me, "I put a fleece out to the Lord saying if you really love me, send Johnny Crump to my house later today." What does that have to do with God's eternal love towards a person? Whether or not Johnny Crump turns up, the man is still loved! God has already declared that He loves us. Fifth, the devil can manipulate and control. It is a good thing that Job was not putting out a fleece when his home and family were wiped out. Some of you have been fleecing for decades and need to rethink God's guidance.

The Medium Effect

A third abuse is the Medium Effect. Have you ever had someone whisper in your ear, "I have a word from the Lord for you"? You might ask, "What is wrong with that? Doesn't the Bible talk about words of wisdom and words of knowledge?" Nothing has to be wrong with that and sometimes a person may have a word from the Lord for us. The onus is on us to weigh this word against scripture and to test it against what God has already said to us.

A "personal word" which is not tested by scripture or weighed against the already-revealed will of God, can end up being, in effect, the words of a medium.

When I am prophesying over people, I often ask the person if there is any rationale to what has been shared. If it is something they are hearing for the first time, I will say, "Do not proceed with this until you get some kind of confirmation." Do not just go on the one word; wait for confirmation. It can be the Spirit speaking in your spirit. It can be the peace of God in your heart that says, "This is right." It might be a truth that emerges from your Bible reading. It may be a door of opportunity opening up to you. I am not going to change my whole life based on one personal prophecy. I need more substance than that. Even the godliest of people can get it wrong.

Let me show you a weird part of the Bible. Acts 20:22 reads, "The Spirit compelled Paul to go to Jerusalem." Then in Acts 21:4 it says, "The Christians at Tyre, through the Spirit, urged Paul not to go to Jerusalem." In Acts 21:10-12 the prophet Agabus warned Paul that he would be bound and arrested if he went to Jerusalem. Finally, Acts 21:13-14 says Paul's answer was, "The Lord's will be done."

However, you want to read that passage, somebody had a bit of bad luck. Either Paul got it wrong, or the Christians in Tyre got it wrong. You have two opposing interpretations of one piece of information. The point I am making is this: if you have received a personal prophecy, that is wonderful. However, do not consider the prophecy as authoritative one its own, because even the most godly people can make a mistake. Tie it together with two other pieces of string, because a cord of three strands is not easily broken.

Five Voices

Now that we have identified some spurious means of

God's direction, we can move on to distinguishing the different voices that speak to us. I want to touch on what I consider the five primary voices.

First, there is the **voice of the world**. The Bible says, *"The whole world is under the control of the evil one."*[136] This voice appeals to our rational mind—it sounds good. In the language of Genesis 3, the forbidden fruit is pleasant to our eyes—it looks good. The confusion comes when the Spirit says, "No deal," but our mind is saying, "What a flippin' great deal!" The world has captivated our thinking by rational, normal assessment.

It has become the controlling influence, rather than the voice of the Spirit. Listening to this voice is something we have all done. And let us be honest, it can be difficult to hear the voice of God when the world is shouting in our ear.

Second, there is the **voice of the flesh**. We feel called to be a missionary in Hawaii. Hey, someone's gotta do it. This voice appeals to desire: the lust of the flesh, the lust of the eyes and pride in what we have and do.[137] In Genesis 2 language, the trees of paradise were *"pleasing to the eye and good for food."*[138] When it comes to hearing the voice of God, you have to learn to crucify your own desires or you will be in a state of confusion.[139] You have to put your desires to death and say, "Not what I want, but what you want." The flesh appeals to the sensual, carnal side. The Bible points out the titanic struggle between the flesh and the Spirit.

I have the desire to do what is good, but I cannot carry it out. For what I do is not the good I want to do; no, the evil I do not want to do—this I keep on doing. Now if I do what I do not want to do, it is no longer I who do it, but it is sin living in me that does it. So I find this law at work: When I want to do good, evil is right there with me.

For in my inner being I delight in God's law; but I see another law at work in the members of my body, waging war against the law of my mind and making me a prisoner of the law of sin at work within my members.[140] The voice of the flesh is smooth and seductive. Do not listen to the flesh. *"Let the Holy Spirit guide your lives. Then you won't be doing what your sinful nature craves."*[141]

Third, there is the **voice of the devil**. This voice appeals to our pride. "If you do this, you will look cool." That is why it is always easier to get people on the worship team than on the cleaning rotation of the church. It is amazing how the will of God works that out. The serpent disclosed to Eve that the forbidden fruit would make her like God! The enemy was massaging the ego of the human personality. The appeal to ego puts life out of focus and clouds what God wants to communicate. Paul lamented to the Corinthians, *"I am afraid that just as Eve was deceived by the devil's cunning, your minds may be led astray."* [142]

Fourth, there is the **voice of the imagination**. This voice appeals to the fanciful in our thought life. It is daydreaming. Perhaps you are like me, I can think of 15 things to do every day. If I drive past an empty building, I have an idea what to do with it. That is how some of us are made.

I remember one time saying to the brothers, "Guys, we need to rent Wembley Stadium and have a teenage prayer meeting. Our society has given up on teenagers. Social services, parents and schools have all given up on them. We need to pull together 80,000 to 90,000 teenagers for a day of prayer and intercession as a prophetic voice to the nation." Everybody thought it was a great idea until some practical brother asked how

much it was all going to cost. "It is so cheap. We can have the whole stadium for the day for £350,000. All we need are lights, staging and sound."

Well, where I come from in Wales, you can buy a whole village for £350,000. Suddenly, the *imaginary* will of God evaporated. It is all right to have great visions. But if you are of that ilk or mindset where you see opportunities all the time, you must submit to the insights of others.

Fifth, there is the **voice of the Holy Spirit**. The interaction between Adam and God in Genesis chapter 2 provides three characteristics of the voice of God. These characteristics will enable us to discern the difference between the other four voices and the voice of God. *"The LORD God placed the man in the Garden of Eden to tend and watch over it. But the LORD God warned him, "You may freely eat the fruit of every tree in the garden— except the tree of the knowledge of good and evil. If you eat its fruit, you are sure to die."* There are three truths to deduce from this passage.

Characteristics of God's Voice

First, God spoke with **authority**. There was an authoritative strength in what God was saying. When the devil spoke to the first couple, it was cunning and deceptive, even a little overpowering. There is a great difference between being spoken to with authority and cunning communication. Remember when you were in school, some teachers had it and some did not. Some ranted and raved and screamed, but there was no authority. In the next class, everything happened like clockwork because there was authority. The voice of God has an authority that is majestic and strong.

Second, the voice of God is **distinctive and clear**. Adam and Eve knew exactly what to do and what *not* to do. God was not fuzzy, hazy or misty. Fuzziness is not a God thing. We need clarity to walk by faith. God provides both the clarity and the substance. He gives us something concrete to base our faith on so we can move forward. I am not saying that He is going to tell us the whole deal. He *will* give us a sufficient understanding to get us to the next stage of the journey.

When I said "yes" to Jesus and the call to ministry at age 16, I did not understand what it would mean to be a minister. I did not know that I would go to 54 different countries.

I had never been out of Wales. God does not reveal the complete picture, but He gives us sufficient information for the current stage of the journey. We often want more information than is necessary. This may be curiosity or it may be a lack of confidence in God. If we have just enough guidance for this stage of the journey, then we are walking by faith.

Third, the voice of God is **comprehensive**. God tells us *what* we need to know *when* we need to know it. For example, in 1982, my car died. I am not mechanically adept, but I know where to put the petrol, the water and the diesel—apparently, diesel cars do not like petrol. There was a garage in south Wales with a Christian owner. He told me to come to his garage and that he would give me a good deal. So I prayed: "God, I do not know what I want or what is good. Lead me." The Lord said two things to me: "Red, 79." I went to the garage and looked around for a red car, but the bloke did not have a red car on the lot. So, I started to move in the flesh a little. I told him that I was looking for a car around 1979. He pulled up a nice car, and, yes, it was a 1979, but it was blue. I took it for a drive. I thought, "Well, we're half way there aren't we? It's a '79 and it's blue—we're half right."

I felt agitated. I said, "You wouldn't have any red cars would you?" I felt like an absolute twit. He said he did not think so, but then his son reminded him about a red car that came in the previous Thursday. It was in the shop being spruced up. I asked if I could look at it. It was a red 1979. I said, "That's the one I want." He said, "You haven't even driven it yet." That was all I needed to know. The two critical pieces of information differentiated it from every other car on the lot.

Developing Our Ability to Hear

How do we develop an ability to hear the voice of God? First, get familiar with **the Bible**. Read the Bible consistently, reverently, regularly and prayerfully. Meditate on it; let it sink into your spirit. *"Solid food is for the mature who by constant use have trained themselves to distinguish good from evil."* [143] When you constantly upload the Word onto your mental hard drive, the vast quantity of truth leaves little or no room for error. Do not seek to know all the errors, know the truth. It is the truth that sets you free. [144] I want to challenge everybody to read the Bible through this year. Get familiar with the Bible, get used to the Bible. You will experience the stage where you stop reading the Bible and the Bible starts reading you.

It is then that you have hit a vein of gold in your mining of scripture.

Second, extend your **fellowship with Jesus**. Do not limit yourself to a 20- or 30-minute devotional time or going to church. Talk to Jesus in the car and walking down the street. Cultivate a constant communion with God.[145] People might think you are weird, but you need to take Jesus into every area of your life.

Third, **be faithful to God**. Make the right choice. When you have to choose between the easy choice and the right choice, always choose right. By practicing obedience to the Lord in basic things, you will find that in difficult choices you have already set a lifestyle pattern where obedience to Jesus is normal. You do not have to go to the altar again; you are already on the altar.[146] You have already counted the cost, whether it is hard or easy. A mindset of obedience tunes your ear to the divine frequency and produces clarity when God is speaking to you.

Fourth, **fast at regular intervals**. Regular fasting kills the fleshly desires of our sinful self. You are saying "no" to fleshy appetites and "yes" to the Spirit. You can practice a partial fast (no meat, no coffee, no TV for a day, a week, a month), or you can prepare for a prolonged fast.

As you go without, you also need to apply yourself to spiritual disciplines. For years, I fasted every Friday. I would go into the church, call upon God, and fill myself with spiritual food instead of natural food. Fasting is a great means for helping us hear the voice of God. As you begin, you may hear nothing at first, but in a while, you will hear. [147]

Fifth, **place faith in what God has said**. Trust the Word of God. Trust the direction that God has shown to you in various ways. When you have tested and discerned the voices speaking to you and have identified the true voice of God, trust it. It will be clear, distinctive, comprehensive or authoritative. If you want that to increase your capacity to hear, you have to be obedient to what God is speaking. Of course, it is scary. No one said it would not be scary. But it is better than being bored.

Hearing the Voice of God:

Study Guide

Flight Plan

Scripture says that "my sheep know my voice." How often do we fail to take that literally in our lives? Now perhaps we will not have the benefit of God's audible voice, but God speaks to us in many ways and it behooves us to discover and yield to his voice in our lives if we really want to live a life of faith. However, we are all familiar with the many voices in our life. Never-mind the voice of peer or social pressure, culture, guilt or shame. Inside of us, our ambitions, ego, dreams or even logic can complicate our ability to discern his voice. In this chapter we gained valuable insight that help us delineate and separate the many voices, so that we hold tightly to the most important one. What comes to mind when you read these statements?

"It is utterly normal for Christians to operate in the

supernatural."

"The issue for us is to discern the difference between the way God gets our attention, and the way in which he speaks."

"The onus is on us to weigh this word against scripture and test it against what God has already said to us."

Take-Off

Hearing God's voice in our life is critical but it is a learning curve as unique as we are. God created us uniquely and knows exactly how to speak to us but we often compare our own experiences with others and judge how God speaks to us as acceptable or not acceptable, valid or not valid based on religious criteria or emotionalism or pride. We have to peel all this back and get right to the root issue. If we have been immersed, baptized into the divine nature, then we have a personal responsibility to learn how to function in the divine nature. We can't leave it someone else, nor can we make the assumption it is not for us. Hearing and discerning

God's leading in our lives is a non-negotiable. We cannot live a life of faith that is pleasing to God without it. In this chapter we explore 3 common misconceptions around hearing God's voice:

1) Misuse of the Bible – using scripture out of context to validate something.

2) The Fleecing Game – demanding God prove his point through obscure means.

3) The Medium Effect – taking the word of another person OVER the word of the Lord to us, or allowing an untested word to lead us.

Have you seen examples of these in your history? Can you dissect what lies you might have believed or misunderstanding you had about yourself or God that influenced this misconception in your life? What have you learned?

Flight Crew

Discussion Questions:

1) When someone says "God Said" what comes to mind?

2) What is the most radical or amazing story you have ever heard of someone following what God said?

3) What concerns or fears come up for you around the idea of God speaking to you?

4) How can you test what you are hearing so you can walk in confidence and faith?

5) What hinders you from moving forward in this?

6) How can you help each other in this journey?

Captain's Log

Reflection: When was a time you know you heard God's voice? How did you know it was him? How often do you invite God to speak to you regarding your decisions?

What have you learned in this chapter that you can apply this week?

Journal Prompt: This week in your journal reflect on the journey of faith you have been on. What is Holy Spirit saying to you in regards to each daily prompt.

Journal: Day 1 What needs to change about how you look at Faith?

Journal: Day 2 What needs to change around my money habits and giving?

Journal: Day 3 What misconceptions have come to light during this time?

Journal: Day 4 What habits, or rhythms do you need to build to walk in more faith and truth?

Journal: Day 5 What can you do to put yourself in a place of regularly hearing from God?

Journal: Day 6 What obstacles or objections come to mind when you consider these changes?

Journal: Day 7 What will you decide? Who will you be accountable to?

In-Flight Training

"By practicing obedience to the Lord in basic things, you will find that in difficult choices you have already set a lifestyle pattern where obedience to Jesus is normal". Choose one basic rhythm or habit that is obedience to something the Holy Spirit has highlighted in the past few weeks and make a plan to practice it this week.

Checking IN or Checking OUT?

Take a moment to listen to your inner dialogue as you consider the commitments you are making. What temptations to "check out" of these commitments do you see? What justification creeps in that allows you not to take this too seriously? What hurry, worry or fear knocks at the door? What power do you have available to you to deal with these enemy tactics? What will you choose when they confront you this week?

Will you check IN or check OUT?

Ground Control

Set some time aside for silence and solitude. Invite your heavenly Father to speak to you by His Holy Spirit. What thoughts bubble up? What is the still small voice whispering to you?

1) Write it down.

2) Test it. (Is it congruent with the nature of God and with scripture?)

3) Make it sacred; do not dismiss it, but take it seriously.

Soaring Higher

Reread pages 343-346. What do you need to do to put these five things into your life?

1) Get familiar with the Bible.

2) Extend your fellowship with Jesus.

3) Be faithful to God.

4) Fast at regular intervals.

5) Place faith in what God has said.

Of course, it is scary. No one said it would not be scary. But it is better than being bored.

Taking New Frontiers

"The person who follows the crowd will usually go no further than the crowd. The person who walks alone is likely to find himself in places no one has ever seen before."[148]

— Albert Einstein

"After the death of Moses, a servant of the Lord, the Lord said to Joshua son of Nun, 'Moses My servant is dead; now then, you and all these people get ready to cross the Jordan River into the land I'm about to give them – to the Israelites. I will give you every place where you set your foot as I promised Moses. Your territory will extend from the desert to Lebanon and from the great river Euphrates, to the Hittite country to the great sea to the west, and no one will be able to stand up against you all the days of

your life. And as I was with Moses so I will be with you. I will never leave you or forsake you.'"[149]

We are living in days when God is doing tremendous things in the earth. At a recent conference, a pastor from Bogotá, Columbia spoke about his church. Four years ago, they had 400 cell groups in their church. In his words, they were struggling along. Now they have 23,600 cell groups. In fact, they no longer count people in the church; they only count cell groups because it is difficult to determine how many people actually belong to the church.

God is doing wonderful things in our world. There are new frontiers to move into so that we can absorb what God wants to do in our life, in our church, in our town and in our country. God is on the move, the breath of His Spirit is moving all over the world, and I am convinced that what God is doing in other parts of the world he wants to do where you are.

Now God only has one method; it is people. To the degree that God is going to move, He is going to do something inside of us to see that take place. We do appreciate and understand the sovereignty of God—where God can do things spontaneously, supernaturally without asking anyone's permission. He just does what He wants to do. But in the normal course of life, He operates, communicates, and cooperates with people who have a heart for Him and what He wants to do in our generation.

I have been a Christian for over 40 years and there has never been a time where it is easier to share your faith in the United Kingdom than it is right now. There has never been a greater openness to talk about Jesus in the entire world than there is right now. There are some incredible initiatives that are taking place and will continue if Jesus does not return. It is important to understand that we need to get on with what God is on with. Did you get that? We need to get on with what God is on with. I want, by the grace of God, to help you to think beyond yourself. I want you to begin to understand that you are to seek God's opportunities.

Seizing a Personal Promise

In Joshua 1:3, the Israelites were given a promise: *"I will give you every place you will set your foot as I promised Moses."* There are many promises in the Bible and, at times, God through His Spirit applies those promises to us personally. At other times, promises come to the corporate Body, or local church. The best opportunities for us to seek are the promises that God has already made to us personally and corporately.

There may be an anointing in the Body for evangelisation or for mission or for training and equipping. We have to ask ourselves, "Where do we fit into that anointing?" Many of us will never be a "full-time Christian worker." Hallelujah for that! You can be a lawyer, a solicitor, a bank manager, a carpenter, teacher, nurse or a refuse collector. If all those jobs are taken, well, then you can be a pastor. Of course, I am only joking. The ministry is a high calling, but God does not place a higher priority on pastors or evangelists than any other calling or profession. All parts of the Body are needed and anointed for service.

Ephesians 4:11, 12 indicates that those called to full- time ministry are specialists, whose primary purpose is to equip the Body—the lawyers, the teachers, the bankers, the daycare workers —to do the work of the ministry. You are a minister, an anointed one, a Christian—a little Christ. Jesus is inside of you.

That means that we need to begin to understand why God made us. We need to bring to mind what God said to us to us in the past about our calling. What has God said to you personally? Many people within the Body of Christ have been wandering around without specific purpose or direction for a long time—like the Israelites who wandered around for 40 years. They were good at doing the general things but not good at doing the specific things. They were terrific at meandering.

Some of us have had our destinies hijacked. Some of us have had our calling quenched. Many go to church, sing the songs, fit into the flow of what is happening, and create an image of being OK, but are doing nothing more than meandering. If we are only OK, we are not OK.

Embracing Your Personal Destiny

Do you know why you are alive? If you could write a mission statement about your life, what would it be? If I could have a personal interview with you, what would you tell me about your life's purpose? What would you come up with?

Many of us think in compartmental terms. We have boxes or pigeonholes for the various parts of our life. But they are kept separate. We think of church and our ministry within the church. We have our social life. Then there is our business life or work. Finally, there is our family life. We have it all nicely compartmentalised, and we are not even schizophrenic.

Life should be approached in a cohesive or integrated fashion. Everything we do should be driving toward the one goal or purpose for which God has made us.

If God has called you to be successful in business, please be successful in business and make a load of cash for the kingdom of God. But some of us have excuses. Some of those excuses are legitimate, but they do not help the cause. You might say, "Ian, I am absorbed with work at the moment." Then I want to ask you about your destiny. First, did God call you to that profession? Second, did God call you to that particular company? Third, are you fulfilling the original mandate that God gave you? It is important to answer these questions, because you will spend 40 or 50 per cent of your life in your profession. It is absolutely imperative that you discover why you were born. Are you fulfilling your God-given destiny?

It is imperative that we move out of our meandering, wandering mindset. If we have made a mistake, God is gracious. Hello! If we have made a mistake, God is gracious. Let me tell you, it is very difficult to move outside the will of God. If you have made a few mistakes, God wants to move you back toward your destiny. He has a vested interest in you. He put His Son on the cross to achieve His ultimate purpose for you. God has a way of making sure you are going to get there *if* you are prepared to work with Him.

A New Worldview

The Israelites had a second problem: they developed a manna mentality. They had been meandering in the desert for 40 years. Through all those years, God had miraculously provided daily sustenance for them. They would open their tent flap and there was breakfast, lunch and tea all in a takeaway bag waiting for them on the sand. They saw Moses as the means to their daily crust. When the water didn't taste good, they complained. When they remembered the taste of leeks and onions, they complained. When they craved the taste of meat, they complained. They had become completely self-centred and self-serving—they had a manna mentality.

Like the Israelites, we can see Christian leaders as a means to *our blessing*. They are there to give us our weekly takeaway blessing. Our pastors are on call to help us with the pain of living. Our cell group leader is there to help us survive the next seven days. If this is how we view leadership, then we have developed a manna mentality. There is a world of difference between believing that the church is there to meet my needs, and believing that the church is there to conquer new territory in obedience to the purposes of God.

Signs of a Manna Mentality

Let me give you some signs of a manna mentality.

a. *Critiquing the worship.* "I just didn't feel blessed because the soprano was flat on that high note!" I just didn't sense the presence of the Lord emanating from the worship team. How am I supposed to feel blessed when the worship is substandard?"

b. *Critiquing the sermon.* "The pastor was a little off today. I just didn't feel the anointing!"

c. *Critiquing the ministry of others.* "Are the needs of my family being met? Do they do something for the toddlers? Is there a decent youth group here?

That is a supermarket mentality. "The church is there to provide quality products and services, and if they aren't up to my standards, I am going to shop—I mean worship— somewhere else!"

Needless to say, this an egocentric, selfish and non- biblical type of Christianity. I want to challenge our attitudes, particularly those of us that have been married for under 10 years and are trying to build homes and raise a family. We face all kinds of different pressures.

We obviously want a healthy church environment for our families. But when we become shoppers rather than worshipers and masters rather than servants, the "me first" manna mentality has taken over.

Write a Family Mission Statement

I want to encourage every couple to write a family mission statement. Write down why you think God brought you together as a couple and what God wants from you as a family. Otherwise, you're just going to turn up at church, learn the new songs, get excited at the excitable points but arrive at 50 years of age wondering, "What have I done with my life?" The destinies of some have been hijacked. I trust that the Holy Spirit will challenge you all over again and that a burning desire will motivate you toward your destiny. When they put us in a box in the ground, and it is all over, the only things left are the things that we have produced for Jesus. It will not matter where we lived, the car we drove, the size of our pension or investments. No, the only thing we leave behind as a legacy is what has been transacted eternally by the grace of God.

New Frontiers

There are times when we suffer or are hindered by the missteps of our forefathers. Moses, though a great man in many ways, blew it and did not take the people into the Promised Land. He had the opportunity, but did not achieve his destiny. It may be that some of us have to move debt out of our lives— the spiritual debt that has accumulated as a result of insensitive leadership, bad leadership, leadership improperly modelled. But let me tell you this, after identifying the problems, you and I have to make the decision to move on!

In Joshua 1:4, there were new frontiers for the Israelites to conquer. Verse 4 says this, "Your territory will extend from the desert to Lebanon and to the great river, Euphrates, to the Hittite country to the great sea to the west." Those were the boundaries. The Lord had said to him, "Every place where you put your foot, I'm going create an opportunity for you to conquer and to take ground."

Joshua was a new breed, a new generation of leader. Have you ever thought about God's instruction to Joshua of putting his foot in certain places? There are certain places we have not taken because we have not put our foot there.

We may have a cool and insipid prayer life simply because we have not put our foot there. We have not moved on in faith because we have been nervous to go beyond our resources.

Listen, we all feel insecure at times. Joshua felt insecure; he was going somewhere he had never been or even seen. I feel insecure when I am taking on a new project or moving into new territory. That is not abnormal, nor is it weird. What is *not* normal is to refuse to move on in faith because we feel insecure. That is weird. You were born to be abnormal, to take new ground in the areas of faith. You do not know that Jesus is the only thing you need, until Jesus is the only thing you have. And you might never discover that until you go beyond your boundaries.

One of my first journeys of faith happened many years ago when I felt that the Lord wanted me to go to America to preach. I prayed about it and spoke to my church leadership and they were happy to see me go. I went, but I only had enough money for a one-way ticket. I am not sure how I even got into the U.S. on a one-way ticket because normally they demand a two-way ticket. When I arrived at my first set of meetings, the brothers who were arranging them thought that I was coming next week. Exciting!

When Jesus is the only person you have, you realise you have nothing else. They put me up in a motel and by the end of the week, my money was absolutely gone. Then the brother that was taking me to the airport was two hours late and I missed my flight.

When I arrived in Dallas/Fort Worth, the meeting had already finished two hours earlier. It was very encouraging. I was 5,000 miles from home thinking, "How the stink do I get out of this?" I attended a church service the following morning and somehow they found out there was a foreigner in attendance. In fact, they called me an *English person.* Can you imagine how insulting that was? After all, I am Welsh. They asked the English person to come and bring a greeting. I gave a greeting and sat down. All I could think was I had to find a way to San Diego and Los Angeles to complete my glorious preaching itinerary. My wallet was still empty and I did not even have a credit card. On my way out of the service, someone came up to me with one of those suspicious brown envelopes. I thought it is either a blessing or a bomb. I picked it up and it felt like a blessing, so I quickly ran to the bathroom and opened the blessing. It was fantastic. There was enough money to get me to Tulsa, LA, San Diego and home to London. There was even enough to buy some gifts!

Boring isn't it? I remember sitting in that church service and thinking, "Jesus, there is no way out. I do not have a credit card; how do we do this?" I sensed a small voice saying, "Just trust me. Just trust me." The Bible says, *"The righteous are going to live by faith."*[150] When you put your foot down, where are you going to put your foot? Is it in the prayer circle? Is it in the faith circle? Where are you putting your foot down? Some of us are so vague that if asked what you need prayer for, you could not even give an answer.

Friends, if you are in a rut, then do something for the first time. When was the last time you did something for the first time? Do something for the first time. Shake yourself, get the adrenaline of faith going again, get the excitement of the unknown going again, get vision pumping again, get a picture of your future again. Stir up the personal promises that God has put over your life. Seize your personal destiny.

Father, there is power and life in Your Word. We believe, Lord, that something eternal will transact in peoples' spirits as Your Word emanates. We pray that You will energise Your Word in us in Jesus' name. Amen.

Taking New Frontiers: Study Guide

Flight Plan

We have a deeper and more clear understanding of what faith is, the generosity through which it is demonstrated, the obedience that is required and the testing that will come. We have practiced discerning the voice of God and how he wants to lead us and we have begun a journey of establishing habits and rhythms that will carry us forward. We have built relationships, shared moments and together we have an opportunity to seize with great courage the road set before us.

God has opportunities waiting for us to say YES to. We don't have to get to the "finish line" before we graduate and become useful for God's Kingdom. Faith is a growth process that is ongoing and ever-increasing, faith is a lifestyle and there is always a next step.

We find ourselves in a position to abandon old ways, religious way and step into a vibrant, real-time relationship with the King of the Universe. He has a plan for world transformation and we get to be a part of it. What stirs up in your spirit when you read these quotes?

"We need to get on with what God is on with. I want, by the grace of God, to help you think beyond yourself. I want you to begin to understand that you are to seek God opportunities."

"We have not moved on in faith because we have been nervous to go beyond our resources."

"You were born to be abnormal, to take new ground in the areas of faith."

Take-Off

Confronting darkness and the enemies lies will be a part of your new rhythm as God invites you on the next steps of your faith journey. This will require leaving some things behind. In this chapter we discovered that we need a new worldview that shakes off the "manna" mentality or consumer mindset that easily besets us.

Take a few moments to reflect on your interactions over the last year at church and with other Christians. Were those interactions about giving or having our needs met? Were we more concerned about being right, or being good?

Were we more focused on other people's behaviour than taking responsibility for our own? How attentive have we been to matters of the heart and mind? Where has religion and ritual been or normal rather than faith and risk?

Flight Crew

Discussion Questions:

1) What have your learned about yourself over this study?
2) Where have you found yourself nervous to move beyond your resources?
3) Where will you put your foot down? Faith circle or prayer circle?
4) What do you need in place to ensure this doesn't settle in your life as information, but actually produces change?
5) How are you going to stick with this once this book is done?

Captain's Log

Reflection: Take time to reflect and write a personal (and family) mission statement.

Journal prompts: Take time to summarise what Holy Spirit has said to you over this journey and put an action plan in place for your next 30 or 60 days.

In-Flight Training

Share your mission statements, summary and action steps with someone who can help you be accountable for the next 30-60 days. When we speak it out, our ears hear it and faith rises up to see it happen in our lives.

Checking IN or Checking OUT?

Take a moment to listen to your inner dialogue as you consider the commitments you are making. What temptations to "check out" of these commitments do you see? What justification creeps in that allows you not to take this too seriously? What hurry, worry or fear knocks at the door? What power do you have available to you to deal with these enemy tactics? What will you choose when they confront you this week?

Will you check IN or check OUT?

Ground Control

Set some time aside for silence and solitude. Invite your heavenly Father to speak to you by His Holy Spirit. What thoughts bubble up? What is the still small voice whispering to you?

1) Write it down.
2) Test it. (Is it congruent with the nature of God and with scripture?)
3) Make it sacred; do not dismiss it, but take it seriously.

Soaring Higher

Who will you invite to read this book?

Will YOU lead the next small group?

What is Holy Spirit saying to you about what is next?

When was the last time you did something for the first time? Shake yourself, get the adrenaline of faith going again, get the excitement of the unknown going again, get the vision pumping again, get the picture of your future again. Stir up the personal promises that God has put over your life. Seize

Endnotes / Bibliography

[1] New Living Translation

[2] Romans 12:3

[3] See Matthew 10:11-13

[4] Matthew 18:19

[5] 2 Corinthians 1:20

[6] See Numbers 13

[7] Hebrews 10:20

[8] Romans 8:31

[9] Thomas Culpepper, QuoteHD.com, 2016 www.quotehd.com/quotes/nicholas-culpeper-scientist-for-gods-sake-build- not-your-faith-upon-tradition-tis", accessed June 25, 2016.

[10] Romans 1:17

[11] Romans 14:23

[12] Romans 3:22

[13] Hebrews 11:27

[14] Exodus 5:1

[15] Joshua 14:7-12 NIV

[16] Joshua 14:7 NKJV

[17] Numbers 13:30

[18] Joshua 14:12 NIV

[19] Hebrews 11:24-25

[20] Hebrews 11:27

[21] 2 Corinthians 4:13 KJV

Chapter 3 – Doubt Your Doubts

[22] Søren Kierkegaard, GoodReads.com, 2016

http://www.goodreads.com/quotes/39173-every-mental-act-is-composed-of- doubt-and-belief-but, accessed June 25, 2016

[23] John 20:31

[24] Romans 1:17

[25] John 2:19

[26] Matthew 12:39-40 New Living Translation

[27] Hebrews 11:6 NLT

[28] Matthew 19:26

[29] Mark 8:31

[30] Matthew 27:62-64

[31] Romans 4:19

[32] Genesis 15:4-6

Chapter 4 – Ever Increasing Faith

[33] Mahatma Gandhi, BrainyQuote.com, Xplore Inc, 2016. http://www.brainyquote.com/quotes/quotes/m/mahatmagan150708.html, accessed June 25, 2016.

[34] Philippians 4:14-20

[35] Luke 6:38

[36] Matthew 19:29

[37] 1 Timothy 6:18-19 The Living Bible

[38] 2 Corinthians 9:11

[39] 1 Timothy 6:17

[40] Psalm 24:1

[41] 2 Corinthians 9:9-11

[42] Romans 14:23

[43] Romans 1:17

Chapter 5 – Maintaining your Confidence

[44] Philippians 3:1-3 New Living Translation

[45] Philippians 3:3 The Living Bible

[46] 1 Samuel 17:45-46 The Living Bible

[47] Special Air Service is the principal special forces unit of the British army

[48] 1 Samuel 17:45-46 The Living Bible

Chapter 6 – Seizing your Destiny

[49] Ephesians 1:1-3 NIV

Chapter 7 – Living Generously

[50] Simone De Beauvoir, wiseoldsayings.com, 2016 http://www.wiseoldsayings.com/generosity-quotes/page-2/, accessed June 25, 2016

[51] Luke 6:38 NIV

[52] 2 Peter 1:4

[53] Colossians 1:13 NLT

[54] Deuteronomy 33:11; Proverbs 6:31 KJV

[55] Matthew 6:21 NIV

[56] Matthew 6:24

[57] Matthew 10:8; Proverbs 11:24

[58] 1 Timothy 6:17

[59] Deuteronomy 14:22-23

[60] Malachi 3:10 NLT

[61] Isaiah 50:7

[62] Proverbs 3:5, 10 NLT

[63] Matthew 6:19-21 NLT

[64] Proverbs 22:9 NIV

[65] Psalm 112:5-6

[66] Psalm 112:5-6

[67] Proverbs 11:25

[68] Acts 11:25 The Message

[69] Matthew 16:25 NLT

Chapter 8 – Waiting for a Miracle

[70] Elisabeth Elliot, Passion and Purity: Learning to Bring Your Love Life Under Christ's Control, Published April 5th 2012 by Fleming H. Revell Company (first published 1984)

[71] 2 Corinthians 11:22-29

[72] Philippians 4:6 The Message

[73] Philippians 4:7 The Message

[74] 1 Peter 5:7 TNIV

[75] 1 Peter 5:7 The Message

[76] Psalm 55:22 NLT

[77] Luke 8:49 NLT

[78] John 16:33

[79] Luke 8:50

[80] 2 Chronicles 20:10-12

[81] 2 Chronicles 20:14,15

[82] Psalm 50, 73-83

[83] Deuteronomy 31:6,8; Joshua 1:5

[84] 2 Chronicles 20:22-26

[85] James 1:18

[86] 2 Timothy 1:7 NLT

[87] Matthew 28:20

[88] 2 Chronicles 20:17,18 NLT

Chapter 9 – The "Whats" of Life

[89] Lee Strobel, BrainyQuote.com, Xplore Inc, 2016. http://www.brainyquote.com/quotes/quotes/l/leestrobel526747.html, accessed June 25, 2016

[90] Hebrews 13:5 NKJV

[91] Matthew 6:15

[92] Matthew 5:11

[93] Luke 3:8

[94] Ephesians 4:26

[95] Matthew 16:18

Chapter 10 – Faith To Walk in Darkness

[96] James 1:2-4 The Message

[97] Isaiah 50:10

[98] John 3:19

[99] Proverbs 26:11

[100] Deuteronomy 11:18; 1 Chronicles 28:9; Matthew 22:37; Romans 12:1-3; Ephesians 4:22-24; Philippians 4:7; Colossians 3:2; 1 Peter 1:13

[101] Ephesians 6:13 CEV

[102] Romans 8:38-39 CEV

[103] Isaiah 50:11

Chapter 11 – What to do When Darkness Falls

[104] Martin Luther King Jr., A Testament of Hope: The Essential Writings and Speeches, Published April 29th 2003 by HarperOne (first published 1986)

[105] Isaiah 50:10

[106] Galatians 6:7 Today's New International Version

[107] Psalm 119:105 NIV

[108] Jeremiah 33:3

[109] Matthew 7:7-8 New Living Translation

[110] See Psalm 37:25; Proverbs 30:8; Matthew 6:11; Philippians 4:19

[111] Philippians 4:6-7 NIV

[112] Jeremiah 23:6; 33:16

[113] Exodus 17:8-16

[114] Exodus 15:22-26; Jeremiah 31:17; Isaiah 61:1

[115] Leviticus 20:8

Chapter 12 – Hearing the Voice of God

[116] Loren Cunningham, topfamousquotes.com, 2016, http:// topfamousquotes.com/quotes-about-hearing-god/, accessed June 25, 2016

[117] 1 Kings 19:9-18 New Living Translation

[118] John 8:47

[119] John 10:27

[120] 1 Corinthians 12:27-28

[121] 2 Peter 1:4

[122] 1 Corinthians 12:13

[123] See 1 Corinthians 12

[124] John 5:24; Romans 6:13

[125] Romans 8:9

[126] Romans 8:14-15

[127] Exodus 19:18

[128] Matthew 28:2

[129] Exodus 13

[130] 1 Kings 18:38

[131] Genesis 3:18

[132] It is the spirit of the believer that is raised to life at conversion. Romans 8:10 says your "spirit is alive because of righteousness." That is, the righteousness of Christ has been imputed to us.

[133] See *George Whitefield,* Volume I, by Arnold Dallimore (Cornerstone Books), pp. 272-3 for a full account

[134] Ecclesiastes 4:12

[135] Romans 14:23 KJV

[136] 1 John 5:19

[137] I John 2:15-17

[138] Genesis 2:9

[139] Galatians 5:24; Romans 8:12,13

[140] Romans 7:18-23

[141] Galatians 5:16 NLT

[142] 2 Corinthians 11:3

[143] Hebrews 5:14

[144] John 8:32

[145] A good example of this principle is found in *The Practice of the Presence of God* by Brother Lawrence.

[146] Romans 12:1-2

[147] If you have never fasted, be sure to get some guidance from a book or your pastor. Fasting has both physical and spiritual benefits. It helps to have a clear understanding about what happens to your body when you fast. It also helps to have clear expectations about the spiritual benefits of fasting.

Chapter 13 – Taking New Frontiers

[148] Albert Einstein, goodreads.com, 2016,

http://www.goodreads.com/quotes/tag/pioneer, accessed June 25, 2016.

[149] Joshua 1:1-5

[150] Romans 1:17

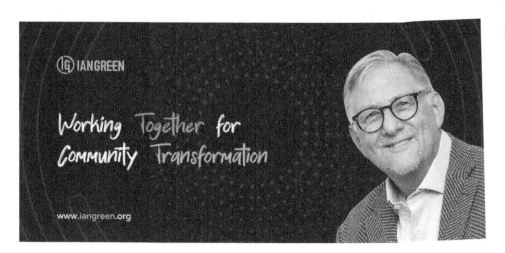

Book Ian Green

Ian has a heart for taking God's vision into action. He travels the world speaking at conferences and seminars, creating and developing networks. He speaks on behalf of the Proton Foundation, sharing the vision and motivating others to step out of their comfort zones and create the life that they are intended to live.

He is a strong and motivational speaker at business events in North America, Europe and Australasia. Ian's guiding values are such that would see businesses and business leaders posture themselves to be solutions in the lives of the widow, poor and orphan.

If you would like to have Ian Green speak at an event, head over to the '***Book Ian Green***' tab on his website:
www.iangreen.org.

 @IanGreen
Communications

 @IanGreen56

 IANGREEN

 @Ian_Green

 @IanGreen

Teaching Resources

Want more encouraging and motivational teaching from Ian Green?

Ian has recorded a number of messages to help individuals equip themselves in their personal, spiritual journey and also in their relational and professional lives. This includes teachings on:

Business • Money • Faith • Christian Life • Leadership • Transformation • Mission

All teachings are available for download (MP3/MP4) or can be ordered as a customised USB.

For information on individual teachings and teaching series, check out:
www.iangreenstore.org

 @IanGreen Communications

 @IanGreen56

 @Ian_Green

 @IanGreen

Printed in Great Britain
by Amazon